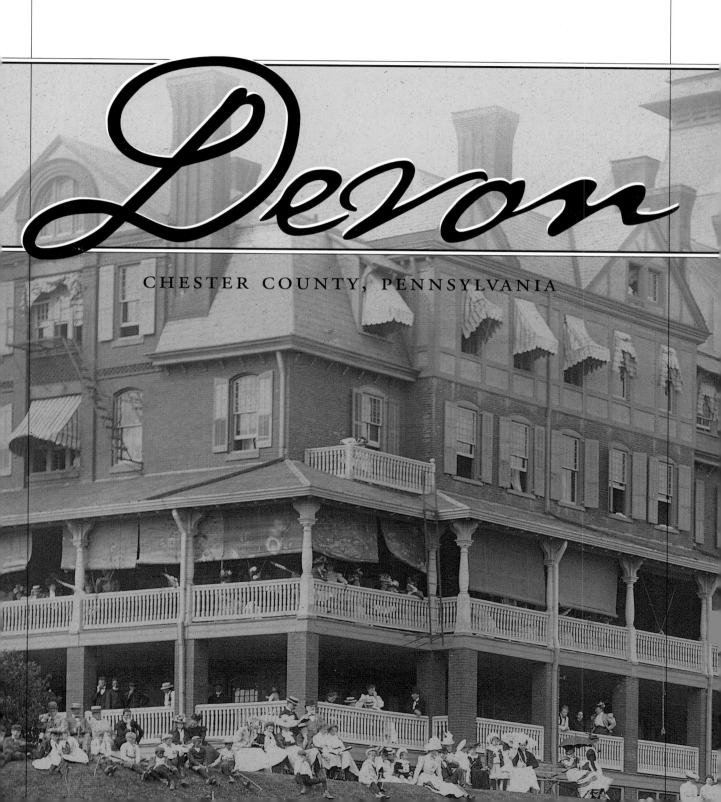

A PICTORIAL HISTORY SHOWING OVER 475 IMAGES

Devon

CHESTER COUNTY, PENNSYLVANIA

▲ Circa 1900 hand painted polo grounds advertisement.

(Courtesy Devon Horse Show and Country Fair, Inc.)

Taken from a speech given in 1966 by local historian, Frances H. Ligget, while presenting her collection of historical data to the Paoli Library:

"Because of the changes taking place in the Valley and the whole area, I feel, that all history should be recorded while there is yet time, and others should be encouraged to carry on this type of project. I consider it like a relay race—with others picking up the torch and preserving our history for other generations who will be grateful to us for doing so."

The authors hope that they have succeeded in "picking up the torch" by preserving in print, the visual aspect of recorded data made by those of whom we are most appreciative. Our thoughts are that you find as much enjoyment in this book as we have.

Enjoy.

ACKNOWLEDGEMENTS

The authors would like to extend a sincere thank you to all who have assisted in making this publication a reality. The many hours devoted to research, scanning, photography, telephone and email conversations, and other, would not have made this book possible without the ongoing support of the following individuals: our spouses; Stacy and Peter; our children, Domenic and Nicholas DiAddezio, Peter, Jr., and his wife, Heather DePiano; Dan DiAddezio; Michael Daniels; Ted Pollard, Radnor Historical Society; Jerry Francis, Lower Merion Historical Society; Pamela Powell, Chester County Historical Society, West Chester, PA; Jack Gumbrecht, R.A. Friedman, The Historical Society of Pennsylvania; Jack Ertell, The Historical Society of the Phoenixville Area; Andrew Jackson, Historical Society of Devon, England; Kati Vamos, Librarian, West Country Studies Library, Devon, England; Warwick Bergin, Peek House, Devon, England; Marylyn Calabrese, Ph.D., writing specialist; Margaret Robinson; Herbert Fry, Easttown Historical Commission; DH2 Design Communications; Gene Williams, Easttown Township; ANRO, Inc.; John W. Beatty; Mons King; Frances Sack, Librarian, Paoli Library; Charlene Peacock, Library Company of Philadelphia; Amy K. Davis, Devon Horse Show and Country Fair, Inc.; Ryan Richards, Bridgett Scott, Suburban and Wayne Times; Bebe Pancoast; Helen Sudhaus; Margay B. Grose; Pat Antrilli; Lou DeStefano; Leslie and Tony Kupstas; Elaine Zappacosta; Ernest C. Eadeh, Eadeh Enterprises; Clifford C. Parker, Chester County Archives & Record Services; Waterloo Gardens; Leslie Phipps; Melissa Purcell; Georgette Cassa; Bernadette Bundy, First Trust Bank, Devon & Berwyn-Devon Business Association; Michael & Becky Wagner; Dan & Heather Hill; Anne Boland; Mr. & Mrs. Ian C. Modelevsky; Bill DeHaven; Mary Ann DiMartini; the late Conrad Wilson; the late Joe Spinelli; the late Martin Spinelli; and, to all those new acquaintances who enlightened our knowledge of Devon, Pennsylvania. ✍

A portion of the net proceeds from the sale of this book will benefit various endeavors which promote history education or awareness and/or historical preservation in our local and surrounding communities—at the authors' discretion.

Designed by: DH2 Design Communications, Berwyn, PA
Printed by: ANRO Inc., Devon, PA

CONTENTS

REDISCOVER DEVON

ÐEVON, named after its counterpart resort town in England, enjoyed the notoriety of being the summer's social mecca of the Main Line for more than three decades. Built within a park-like setting in 1882, The Devon Inn, encircled by the English-named roads of Berkley, Waterloo, Chester and Dorset, had amenities only the wealthy at that time could afford.

Occupying the guests' leisure time, activities and attractions such as golf, billiards, lawn tennis, fox hunting, polo, horseback riding, horse racing, and theatricals, were then considered quite fitting for this suburban Philadelphia resort. The inn's orchestra was always performing, and guests' dancing on the piazzas at any time during the day wasn't an unusual sight. The resort became so popular that the summer season of operation was extended well into the fall.

The energy-filled environment usually associated with an inn of this size came to an abrupt end when the wooden-clad structure was destroyed by fire in 1883. Plans were set into motion to rebuild another inn by the following summer season. Built entirely of stone and brick for fire protection, the new inn was in the same English style as the first, but on a grander scale. Within two blocks of the inn, a spring-fed lake was built to accommodate the fishing and boating activities of the resort. Complete with an elevator and more amenities than one could ever imagine, the inn opened as scheduled in 1884.

The grand reopening ceremony included 600 of the most wealthy and influential citizens of Philadelphia and its surrounding neighborhoods and included officers of the Pennsylvania Railroad. A snapshot of names from one of the early guest registers included Theodore Kitchen, cashier of Philadelphia's Central National Bank; Briton Cox, coal dealer; E.O. McClellan, superintendent of the Eastern Division of the Pennsylvania Railroad; E.H. Frishmuth, tobacco dealer; Robert Glendenning, banker; and Dr. A.R. Thomas, a leading homeopathic physician of Philadelphia. The occupations of these guests clearly indicated the level of wealth that routinely patronized the resort.

The concept of owning a vacation home on a resort or golf course wasn't a novel idea at that time to the patrons of the Devon resort. Large summer cottages and manor homes soon dotted the landscape surrounding the inn after parcels of land, once part of the 40-acre golf course became available for sale.

In 1896, a "Meeting of the Gentlemen" involving local businessmen and area horsemen, was arranged at the inn to discuss a new horse show event that would encourage area farmers to breed good harness horses. The Devon Horse Show Association was organized and held its first one-day event on the inn's racetrack and polo field, the same site as today's show. Henry Coates, partner in the firm of Porter & Coates, publishers of children's books, was the president of the first show in 1896. The 1898–1900 shows grew into two-day events and were held on the inn's spacious lawn, allowing spectators to watch from the wrap-around porches.

For unknown reasons, the show was in hiatus from 1901–1909. In 1910, through the efforts of William T. Hunter, a local Devonite, the show regained its exposure by returning to the polo fields in a three-day horse show event with John T. Windrim as the show's president. William H. Wanamaker, Jr., of the department store family, played a part in organizing the fund that allowed proceeds from a scaled-down 1918 wartime show to be donated to the war's Emergency Aid Effort. Following the end of the war, the show continued its growth and popularity and selected the Bryn Mawr Hospital as the beneficiary for the donations.

▼ Spectators' attire wasn't very casual during the early years of the show. It was required that ladies wear white gloves and a hat while attending the show. Hats worn by ladies at today's shows are reminiscent of a tradition that dates back to a time when it was improper to attend the show unless you wore a hat.

(Circa 1910 photo courtesy Devon Horse Show and Country Fair, Inc.)

Originating from its humble beginning as a one-day event, the Devon Horse Show and Country Fair, Inc. has grown into a ten-day national event attracting over 100,000 spectators and participants from around the world.

With the invention of the automobile, the 30-year-old Main Line resort began its decline. This new mode of transportation gave the Devon guests a faster route to newfound interests in seashore and mountain attractions. The resort era, along with its economic contributions to the community, finally ended in 1913.

After a series of transactions and vacancies, the inn's structure was purchased in 1919, and reopened as The Devon Manor, a school for girls. The school entered into bankruptcy and closed in 1924. In 1926, the once famous inn reopened as The Devon Park Hotel. Even the popularity of the roaring twenties wasn't enough to make this Main Line attraction as successful as the famous Devon Inn. Within two years, the hotel closed its doors. In 1928, the structure was sold to the Valley Forge Military Academy Realty Corporation. After some remodeling, the building opened as the original home to the Valley Forge Military Academy. The academy enjoyed its time in Devon for only a few months, when in January 1929, a disastrous fire destroyed the building once again. Instead of rebuilding on the same site, the academy moved to neighboring Wayne and built a new school.

The Devon Inn resort and the enterprises that followed were the only viable means of economic support to the small town. The military school fire put this Main Line community in jeopardy of losing its existence when the only source of income and employment was reduced to ashes. Even some country cottages and manor homes gave way to a state of disrepair and were boarded up, most likely because the wealthy owners experienced a financial struggle as well.

The generations of Devonites, mostly Italian and Irish immigrants, used their heritage of a strong work ethic and family unity to get them through the economic hardships of a depressed economy. During the 1930s and

beyond, Devon began to prosper once again with businesses and industries moving into its community. With an upsurge in estate homebuilding, Devon regained its status of attracting wealth to its community. Within a short period of time, year-round residents soon occupied those cottages and manor homes that were once used only as summer retreats.

Originating from its humble beginning as a one-day event, the Devon Horse Show and Country Fair, Inc. has grown into a ten-day national event attracting over 100,000 spectators and participants from around the world. This once-a-year show has existed in the same location for more than 100 years and is the only surviving venue from the resort era.

Devon's legendary history is bound to its developers, Lemuel Coffin and Joseph B. Altemus. These two Philadelphia merchants had the ingenious wisdom in the 1880s to transform an area of open fields and farmland into a thriving recreational retreat town that catered to an affluent class in society for more than 30 years. Their ingenuity began Devon's journey of continuous success in attracting wealth and opportunity to its highly desirable community located on the very popular Main Line. ➷

▲ The inn included more conveniences and comforts than one could ever imagine. Complete with an elevator, its many levels and outbuildings could provide well over 300 sleeping suites. Some accommodations included a dining room and parlor while many of the rooms included private baths. Gas was used for lighting, and on occasion, for steam heat.

The water supply for the inn came from an abundance of springs located within the surrounding area. A special pumping station was erected behind the inn to pump water throughout the building and to adjacent structures. To protect the second inn from another fire, an elaborate sprinkler system for its time was connected to a water tank hidden in the inn's cupola. Spigots connected at the ends of each pipe that ran from the tank into the rooms could be turned on to flood the area in the event of fire.

Built into the knoll under the first floor side porch, was a large in-door playground for children. This area included many of the inn's adult amenities that kept the children's nannies and nurses quite comfortable.

(Early 1900 postcard and 1890s sketches courtesy Stephen DiAddezio)

THE RESORT ERA

ESCAPING the summer heat and crowded conditions of Philadelphia, wealthy socialites came to Devon's countryside retreat town to enjoy the quaint setting and refreshing climate. Cool breezes and leisure living kept the Devon Inn open well into the fall. In vogue with the latest fashions of the time, the men and women were always attired in their finest. The inn's first-class laundry made its services available to the guests at all times.

▶ **"All Aboard" at The Devon Inn**
In 1904, a driver and his dog await to transport the inn's elite clientele.
(Courtesy Chester County Historical Society)

Musically accomplished women enjoyed playing the piano for lady guests in their palatial parlors, while the men retired to their exclusive smoking parlors to exchange viewpoints on political happenings, fox hunts and polo matches, or any other activity offered by the inn. It was locally known that the guests played a round of golf at least once every day, and twice on Sundays.

Lavish meals adorned the ever-changing menu. The kitchen chef came from the then-famous Delmonico's in Philadelphia and had access to the inn's 20-acre farm, located nearby for fruits and vegetables. Large parties and events such as the Horse Show Ball successfully proved to be culinary adventures.

By catering to the wealthy in a luxurious fashion for more than 30 years, this grand inn and the venues attached to it, truly earned the notoriety as being the social center of the Main Line.

(Circa 1885 photo courtesy Stephen DiAddezio)

▶ The redesigned structure at the intersection of Berkley and Waterloo Roads in 2007.

(Photo by Peter DePiano, Jr.)

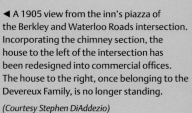

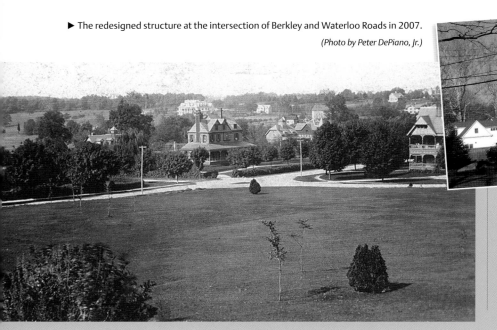

◀ A 1905 view from the inn's piazza of the Berkley and Waterloo Roads intersection. Incorporating the chimney section, the house to the left of the intersection has been redesigned into commercial offices. The house to the right, once belonging to the Devereux Family, is no longer standing.

(Courtesy Stephen DiAddezio)

▲ Built around 1884, the shaded boardwalk bordered Devon Boulevard. The walkway protected the guests' clothing from dirt roads.

(Courtesy Radnor Historical Society)

▲ A view from the Devon Train Station around 1900. The main road connecting the train station to the inn was referred to as The Boulevard. Lancaster Avenue, then-named Arlington Avenue, is in the foreground. To accommodate more guests, the inn built cottages along the side of the boulevard .

(Courtesy Stephen DiAddezio.)

◄ The Boulevard in 2007. When the resort was first designed in 1882, the Boulevard was named Cottage Avenue.

(Photo by Peter DePiano, Jr.)

► An early view from the inn to the Devon train station.
(Circa 1909 postcard courtesy Herb Fry)

►► A 2007 view from Devon Boulevard to the station.
(Photo by Peter DePiano, Jr.)

▲ The portico on the Dorset Road side of the inn provided shelter from the elements for the arriving and departing guests. The 700 feet of wrap-around porches added to the comfortable setting of this fashionable inn.

(Photo courtesy Radnor Historical Society)

▶ A view looking towards Lancaster Avenue from one of the inn's porches.

(Circa late 1890s photo courtesy Radnor Historical Society)

◀ A view of the inn and surrounding area around 1905. This photo may have been taken from The Highland Boarding House, located on Highland Avenue in Devon. The Devon Inn traditionally maintained its full capacity of guests while The Highland provided boarding for 30 additional guests that the inn couldn't accommodate.

(Courtesy Stephen DiAddezio)

◀▼ A rear view of the inn from the intersection of Waterloo and Chester Roads. The four-story laundry and water tower were located at the rear of the inn. Rooms on the upper floor of the laundry were used as sleeping quarters for servants and for storage. An engine building that pumped water to the facilities was situated alongside the laundry. The billiards and game building was located along Dorset Road behind the inn. The inn's swimming pool was believed to be in either the lower level of the laundry or billiards building.

(Courtesy Stephen DiAddezio)

▶ The typical menu at the inn consisted of every type of food the market could provide. The inn's 20-acre farm provided the vegetables and fruits to complement the menu.

One early morning in 1902, the inn's entire service staff, excluding the chef, went on strike. With tarnished pride and ravenous appetites, the elite guests had no choice but to enter the kitchen and serve themselves. The strike was short-lived after management met with the unhappy staff to resolve the issues. By noon, the day continued as though the service to the guests was never interrupted.

(Courtesy Radnor Historical Society)

▲ The dining room, large enough to accommodate all the guests at one sitting, used only the finest linens, china and silverware. A flexible breakfast schedule was provided from 7 a.m. to 11 a.m. to accommodate the morning activities of the guests. Lunch was promptly served at 1 p.m., and dinner later in the day at 6 p.m.; appropriately attired guests filled the dining room to enjoy a two-hour dinner.

(Courtesy Chester County Historical Society)

▶ The entrance lobby provided an ideal location for business transactions dealing with Devon's expanding resort town as well as managing the events, activities, and large array of amenities the resort had to offer. The gentlemen guests also utilized this area to direct their Philadelphia businesses while enjoying the relaxed atmosphere of the inn.

The Devon Inn not only served as the social hub for resort living, but also as a town center for the new community.

(Courtesy Radnor Historical Society)

◄ Connected to the inn by a lobby, a 50 x 70 foot ballroom was added in 1893. Octagonal windows with plush seating flanked both sides of the room. The walls were paneled in pine, and maple wood was used for the dance floor. Commonly seen in European castles and places of parliament in the U.S. and abroad, malachite, a polished blue-green color stone with a distinctive swirl pattern was applied to the ceiling. During the resort era, the ballroom hosted many performances by the Devon Dramatic Association, dances, balls and other events associated with the upscale clientele.

(Courtesy Chester County Historical Society)

The main corridor of the inn ran the entire width of the structure, which was about 334 feet. Windows located at each end provided cool gentle breezes to this country hilltop retreat.

▲ Located on the first floor, a typical gentleman's parlor was decorated in generous proportions. Scenes that kept the sportsman in mind embellished the drapery fabrics. The ladies' parlors were elegantly decorated with fine wallpapers, large mirrors and paintings, and raw silk fabrics adorned the upholstered furniture.

(Courtesy Stephen DiAddezio)

◄ The main corridor of the inn ran the entire width of the structure, which was about 334 feet. Windows located at each end provided cool gentle breezes to this country hilltop retreat.

(Courtesy Radnor Historical Society)

Musical Programme

DEVON INN ORCHESTRA

GEORGE R. COLGAN, Director

Dinner

1776

DEVON INN
DEVON PENNA.

1911

A. STANLEY STANFORD

▼ ▼ Adding to the festivities of the July 4, 1883 celebration, the guests at the inn took up a collection to employ the Phoenix Military Band from Phoenixville. The band performed at community and state events, as well as at veterans' funerals. Originally founded as a community band in 1847, the band later volunteered as a group at the onset of the Civil War and served in the Union Army. They were the first band to be sworn into federal service as part of the 2nd Regiment of the Pennsylvania Volunteers. The band performed well into the 20th century.

(Circa 1897 photo courtesy The Historical Society of the Phoenixville Area)

▼ Early records indicate that in 1882, the inn obtained its ice during the winter months from the Waterloo Mill pond, and stored it there near the dam until an icehouse could be built exclusively for the inn's summer use. An icehouse was later built within close proximity to the inn, and ice cut from the resort's man-made lake during the winter provided a good supply for the summer season. After an artesian well was discovered on the property, the icehouse had to be enlarged to accommodate the increased needs of the inn, as well as those of the surrounding residents.

(Circa 1910 advertisement courtesy The Suburban and Wayne Times)

ICE, 10c. per Hundred

Beautiful, clear, firm Ice, made from pure, artesian well water, 10c. per hundred pounds, at the plant.

DEVON INN,
DEVON, PA.

A. Stanley Stanford.

The capacity of the Ice Plant has now been increased by 2 tons.

▲ The Devon resort held the largest July 4th celebration in the area. The inn portrayed patriotism at its finest by being fully decorated with traditional red, white and blue buntings while the orchestra performed patriotic music throughout the day. The day's festivities included old-fashioned activities like sack and wheelbarrow races, hurdle jumping, bonfires, and a grand fireworks display later in the evening. Over the years, the fireworks grew into a magnificent pyrotechnic display interspersed with musical renditions performed by the inn's orchestra. By 1890, the display attracted more than 2400 spectators from Philadelphia and its surrounding areas. Additional passenger cars had to be added to the train station's schedule to accommodate the popularity of the celebration.

(Circa 1911 program courtesy Chester County Historical Society)

OLD ST. DAVIDS

◄ The old St. Davids church offered the guests staying at the inn not only another place to worship, but also a nearby historic place to visit. Carriages of sightseers often rode along the roads that led to the final resting place of Anthony Wayne.

(Circa 1888 photos of St. Davids Church and worshipers courtesy Radnor Historical Society)

◄ ▼ In 1893, the town's developers donated two parcels of land on Berkley Road to build a Devon chapel and school. That chapel later became known as St. John's Presbyterian Church. The Catholic Italian immigrants who came to Devon to work as gardeners on large estates or in nearby quarries were invited to worship at St. John's on Saturday evenings.

(Circa 1930 photo courtesy Chester County Historical Society)

◄ ▼ ▼After years of holding their worship services at St. John's Presbyterian Chapel in Devon, the Catholic congregation moved to a permanent location on Old Eagle School Road around 1908. Established as Our Lady of the Assumption Church, worshipers proudly pose in front of their new church. The early church has since been replaced on the original site.

▲ The Japanese Floral Café was located on the porch of the inn. Guests and visitors could purchase souvenirs and postcards from the café kiosk, have a meal, or enjoy a cup of tea in the pleasant surroundings. Wednesday's Tea was a popular affair.

(Courtesy Stephen DiAddezio)

▶ A 1900 inn postcard advertised an extensive list of attractions.

(Courtesy Stephen DiAddezio)

Devon Inn, Devon, Pa.
MAY TO DECEMBER
In Beautiful Chester Valley

POST CARD

ADDRESS

SOCIAL CENTER OF THE MAIN LINE

ATTRACTIONS

Devon Horse Show	Horse Show Ball
Polo Matches	Spring Flower Show
Kennel Show	Golf and Tennis
Rose Tree Horse Show	Private Theatricals
Belmont Trotting Events	Bal Masque
Chesterbrooke Races	Autumn Flower Show
Bryn Mawr Horse Show	Auto Exhibition
Devon Fancy Cattle Show	The County Ball

Devon Inn's beautiful Japanese Floral Cafe

¶ Situated amid magnificent Private Estates, Devon Inn enjoys an international reputation for excellence and the high standard of its patronage. ¶ Within a few miles of many points of historical interest, including Signal Hill, Paoli, old St. David's Church, Valley Forge Park and Revolutionary Battle Ground.

A. STANLEY STANFORD, Proprietor
K. RUSH, Associate Manager

▶ Spring and fall flower shows were delightful events at Devon, as well as the Peasant's Market, where locals could display and sell their goods to the guests at the inn.

(Vintage Peasant's Market tag courtesy Chester County Historical Society)

Telephone 784   WE DELIVER

Devon Pharmacy

J. HARTZELL O'LOUGHLIN, Ph.G.

LINCOLN HIGHWAY   DEVON, PENNA.

▼ In the late 1880s, the guests staying at the inn were able to shop at the Devon stores, which were conveniently located nearby. The store pictured below was the Devon drug store and post office with Joseph Rex serving as druggist and postmaster from 1887–89. The American Stores Co. pictured in the middle, was the beginning of what is known today as the ACME Markets. The structure no longer exists.

(Courtesy Chester County Historical Society)

▲▲ Circa 1900 view from Waterloo Road
of the Devon Inn.

(Courtesy American Premier Underwriters, Inc.)

▶ Circa 1910 views of the Devon train station
and underpass.

(Courtesy Stephen DiAddezio)

Devon, Pa.   Penna. R. R. Station

Waterloo Road and Railroad Bridge, Devon, Pa.

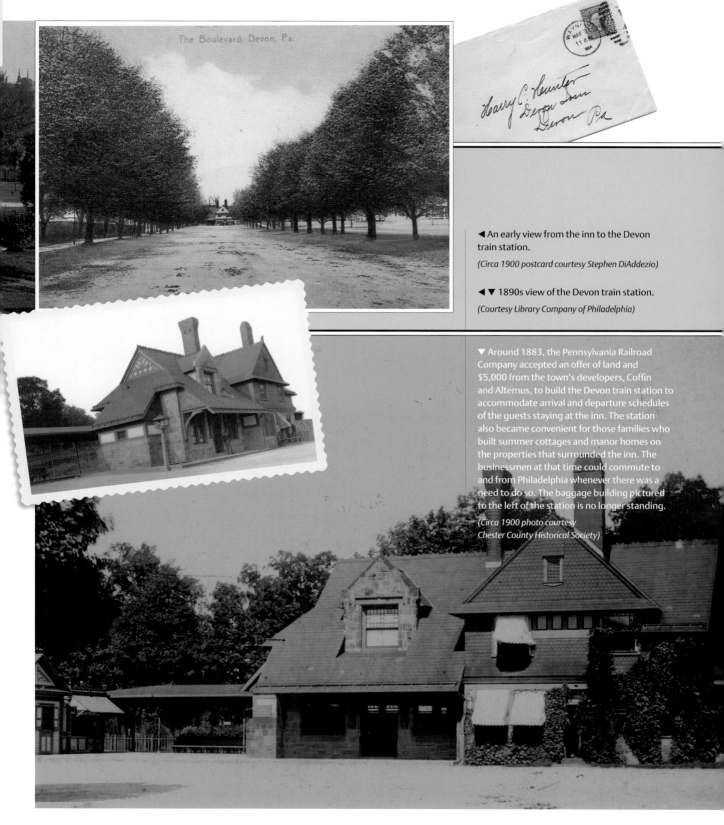

The Boulevard, Devon, Pa.

◀ An early view from the inn to the Devon train station.

(Circa 1900 postcard courtesy Stephen DiAddezio)

◀▼ 1890s view of the Devon train station.

(Courtesy Library Company of Philadelphia)

▼ Around 1883, the Pennsylvania Railroad Company accepted an offer of land and $5,000 from the town's developers, Coffin and Altemus, to build the Devon train station to accommodate arrival and departure schedules of the guests staying at the inn. The station also became convenient for those families who built summer cottages and manor homes on the properties that surrounded the inn. The businessmen at that time could commute to and from Philadelphia whenever there was a need to do so. The baggage building pictured to the left of the station is no longer standing.

(Circa 1900 photo courtesy Chester County Historical Society)

▶ The two structures as pictured in 2007, occupy the same location as the former stables.

▶▶ Around 1890, the second stable facility for the Devon Inn was built alongside the original one. Different in design from its neighboring stable, the new stable accommodated an interior courtyard for additional ventilation and better use of daylight. Buggy storage on the second floor utilized the same hoist system as its neighbor, as well as second floor sleeping quarters for the stablemen.

In 1897, title transferred from Lemuel Coffin to George H. Earl, Jr. and his wife, and Richard Y. Cook and his wife. Shortly after, the property transferred to Annie M. Sullivan, wife of Dennis O. Sullivan.

(1885 architectural drawing courtesy Stephen DiAddezio)

▶ The two-story Devon Inn Stables were built north of the inn opposite Dorset Road on Lancaster Avenue to accommodate the horses and carriages belonging to the guests as well as those used by the inn. A recollection from a local at the time tells about a particular female guest staying at the inn who brought along nine horses and nine carriages of varied sizes and purpose, as well as her overabundance of personal servants.

The stables provided top-of-the-line stalls, complete with iron gates and troughs. The second level housed coachmen, grooms, and hostlers, as well as storage for carriages hoisted up by a pulley system. The stable's exterior wall construction consisted of large, three-inch thick slabs of slate, which fitted into grooved posts. This type of construction allowed the stable configuration to be easily altered to fit the ever-changing needs of its patrons. The structure is no longer standing.

(Circa 1885 photo courtesy Radnor Historical Society)

▶ The inn's stables provided open space for equestrian groups to play and practice. In 1884, a Rosemont club of gentlemen riders moved their group from Rosemont to the 300-acre tract of land in Devon.

George Gould, son of the famous New York financier, Jay Gould, brought his champion polo team to the Devon grounds. Polo was a popular sport to play and observe for the businessmen staying at the inn. The men found pleasure in relating the principles of polo's fast and strategic maneuvers to their business boardroom tactics back in Philadelphia.

(George Gould polo print courtesy Library of Congress Prints and Photographs Division, ggbain-02479)

◀ The old stable property was purchased more than 100 years later around 1990. The structure was transformed into office and retail space while retaining similar architectural lines of the building's former existence. It is not certain if the courtyard was enclosed at one point in time. The pulley system that once hoisted buggies to the second floor was maintained as an interior reminder of past occupancy.

(Circa 1990s photograph courtesy Ernest C. Eadeh, Eadeh Enterprises)

◀ The Ogden School, located on Church Road in Devon, served the children of Waterloo Mills from around 1855 to 1922. The old school is currently a private residence.

In 1893, Easttown Township formed their first high school. Three years later, the class of five students graduated.

Easttown Faculty 1908

◀ In 1893, Easttown Township formed their first high school. Three years later, the class of five students graduated. In 1897, Tredyffrin formed their high school. Within a few years, Tredyffrin utilized the entrance exam from Haverford College as their school's final examination. In 1908, the Tredyffrin and Easttown Joint High School was established.

(Circa 1908 Easttown faculty photo courtesy John W. Beatty)

◀▼ Built in 1854, the Leopard School served as a school, community assembly hall, and a place to hold church services. The school was damaged by fire.

▼ The one-room Leopard School was built in 1882, and remains today in its original location as part of a comfortable home named *Recess*.

(Circa 1925 one-room Leopard School photo courtesy Chester County Historical Society)

1882

▶ An invitation requesting a "Meeting of the Gentlemen" at the Devon Inn, to discuss a new horse show event that would encourage area farmers to breed good harness horses was sent to local businessmen and area horsemen. The Devon Horse Show Association was organized at that meeting and held its first one-day event in 1896 on the inn's racetrack and polo field, the same site as today's show. Many family names of the initial organizers as listed on the invitation have been instrumental in building the area's history and continue to do so.

(Invitation courtesy Chester County Historical Society)

▶ The two-day affair in 1898 attracted entries from West Chester and Lionville. The judges' area was located under a striped canvas awning in the center of the fenced oval, which was situated on the inn's side lawn along Waterloo Road.

According to written accounts, the event on the lawn of the inn not only provided guests with a better view of the show, but also gave the unattached female guests a social environment to have acquaintances with rugged equestrian handsmen and horse owners holding the same availability status as their own. The horse show's popularity grew over the years, and so did the social scene.

*(1898 photo courtesy
Devon Horse Show and Country Fair, Inc.)*

▼ The Breeder's Gazette advertisement.
(Courtesy Stephen DiAddezio)

DEAR SIR:

In order to effect an organization for the purpose of holding a Horse Show at Devon, a meeting of gentlemen, interested in the breeding, showing and ownership of horses, is called for Friday Evening, May 22, 1896, eight o'clock, at Devon Inn.

Please attend and invite others who may be interested.

Signed,

HENRY T. COATES
C. DAVIS ENGLISH
HENRY M. WARREN
GEORGE H. EARLE, JR.
JOHN W. PATTON
D. B. SHARP
LEM. COFFIN ALTEMUS
JOSEPH F. PAGE
R. PENN SMITH
E. B. COLKET
JAMES W. PATTERSON
E. W. TWADDELL

▶ In 1896, Henry T. Coates, partner in the firm of Porter & Coates, publishers of children's books, was the president of the first show. The 1898-1900 shows grew into a two-day event and were held on the inn's spacious lawn, allowing spectators to watch from the wrap-around porches.

(Circa 1898 photo of the children's class of riders courtesy Devon Horse Show and Country Fair, Inc.)

▶ In 1896, Barclay H. Warburton was one of three judges at the first horse show held on The Devon Inn's racetrack/polo grounds. Warburton was educated at the University of Pennsylvania and Oxford University. When his father died in 1884, he assumed his father's position as editor and publisher of the Philadelphia Daily Evening Telegraph, which was founded by the senior Warburton.

In the early 1890s, Warburton met Sarah Dickson Lowrie, a Philadelphia socialite, who was an advocate for public bathhouses. Warburton used his newspaper as a campaign avenue to raise $50,000 to establish and build The Public Baths Association of Philadelphia. The campaign was a success and Warburton held the position of chairman to the finance committee and later vice-president of the association. Warburton married Mary "Minnie" Wanamaker, daughter of John Wanamaker, department store founder.

(Circa 1888 photo courtesy Devon Horse Show and Country Fair, Inc.)

◄ A class of young drivers waiting to be judged at the 1898 show. Helen Hope Montgomery (Scott) participated in the early shows as a young child. Her association with the Devon event lasted more than 60 years, with 23 of those years serving as executive vice-president of the show.

(Courtesy Devon Horse Show and Country Fair, Inc.)

The 1898–1900 shows grew into a two-day event and were held on the inn's spacious lawn, allowing spectators to watch from the wrap-around porches.

▲ Circa 1898 photo of a spectator's view from the inn. There were more than 100 entries from local farms and estates.

(Courtesy The Historical Society of Pennsylvania)

▲ A class of drivers lined up for judging at the 1898 show.

(Courtesy Devon Horse Show and Country Fair, Inc.)

▲ The three-day 1910 show was held for the first time over the Memorial Day weekend. In 1913, the show attracted more than 1000 entries. The area around the oval became so crowded that spectators had to find seating in the bandstand, a distance from the happenings of the inner circle.

(Courtesy Devon Horse Show and Country Fair, Inc.)

▲ Barclay Warburton, Dr. Thomas E. Parkes, and M. Peach were judges at the 1896 show. As the popularity of the horse show increased, so did the number of officials.

(Courtesy Devon Horse Show and Country Fair, Inc.)

▲ Driver and rider class competitions for ladies continue to be as popular today as in 1896.

(Courtesy Devon Horse Show and Country Fair, Inc.)

▲ A class of young riders in 1898 awaiting judge's decision. Ribbons were given as awards, as well as $10 prizes for first place winners in each class and $5 for second place. The monetary prizes were usually given to owners of local farm horses.

(1898 photo courtesy Devon Horse Show and Country Fair, Inc.)

▲ A display of "Brood Mares with Foals at Foot" was a class in the 1898 show on the lawn of the inn.

*(Photo courtesy
Devon Horse Show and Country Fair, Inc.)*

◄ Always in vogue with the latest fashions of the time, the spectators at the show were appropriately attired.

(Courtesy Devon Horse Show and Country Fair, Inc.)

The Devon Horse Show Association

❋

Devon, Chester County, Penna.

Feb, 9th 190*4*

Mrs. H. H. Taylor.

SIR :—

   Your name has been suggested as being one who is interested in the subject, and you are therefore invited to become an active member of this Association.

   The object of the Association is to encourage on proper lines the breeding of horses in this and adjoining counties.

   Our active membership is limited, and we would ask you to give us the benefit of your coöperation. There will be special privileges extended to active members.

   The annual dues are $5.00, and are payable upon your acceptance of this invitation to Charles E. Coxe, Treasurer, Malvern, Pennsylvania.

   Trusting you will give your interest and support in this matter, we are

   Very Respectfully Yours,
   THE DEVON HORSE SHOW ASSOCIATION.

▲ Wearing pretty bonnets is a time-honored tradition at today's show.

(Circa 1910 photo courtesy Devon Horse Show and Country Fair, Inc.)

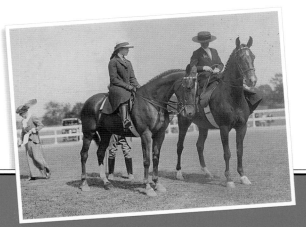

◄ A class of lady riders in 1910. Young girls were allowed to ride in a cross saddle fashion, while adult ladies had to conform to the then-traditional way of riding sidesaddle.

(Photo courtesy Devon Horse Show and Country Fair, Inc.)

Wearing pretty bonnets is a time-honored tradition at today's show.

▲ The only way for a lady to ride in early shows was sidesaddle. Around 1915, some lady riders made a controversial move towards riding cross saddle (astride). Needless to say, the judges disallowed the move until years later when the class was changed to include the previously considered controversial style of mounting.

(Circa 1910 photo courtesy Devon Horse Show and Country Fair, Inc.)

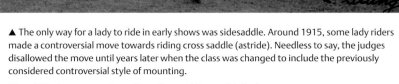

▲ The carriage marathon around 1910.

(Photo courtesy Devon Horse Show and Country Fair, Inc.)

▲▲ A young class of drivers competing in the 1910 show.

(Photo courtesy Devon Horse Show and Country Fair, Inc.)

◄ William T. Hunter standardized prices for stabling and feed at all local stables when he became chairman of the show in 1913. As a way to accommodate the increase in entries at the show, especially for those that came from a distance, Mr. Hunter put his own horses out to pasture and volunteered the empty space in his nearby horse barn for stabling.

Known by locals as the unofficial Mayor of Devon, Mr. Hunter was always visible in promoting the town's interests and growth opportunities. He was involved in any effort at any level of community interest, whether it was first to arrive at the scene of a fire, or allowing free swimming at the pool he built on his Devon property for the local children. Often referred to as Mr. Devon, William T. Hunter was without a doubt, a leading citizen for his time.

*(Circa 1910 photo courtesy
Devon Horse Show and Country Fair, Inc.)*

▼ In 1910, a four-section grandstand of bleachers, covered in sections by a canvas awning, was erected for the comfort of the spectators. The covered sections consisted of the original 46 Devon box seats reserved only for individuals of Philadelphia's highest society. A wood boardwalk covered the area in front of the stands to protect the spectators' clothing from mud in the event of rain.

*(Circa 1910 photo courtesy
Devon Horse Show and Country Fair, Inc.)*

▶ For unknown reasons, the show was in hiatus from 1901-1909. In 1910, through the efforts of William T. Hunter, a local Devonite, the show regained its exposure by returning to the polo fields in a three-day horse show event with John T. Windrim as the show's president.

(Circa 1910 photo courtesy Devon Horse Show and Country Fair, Inc.)

▼ A young rider posing at the 1910 show.

(Photo courtesy Devon Horse Show and Country Fair, Inc.)

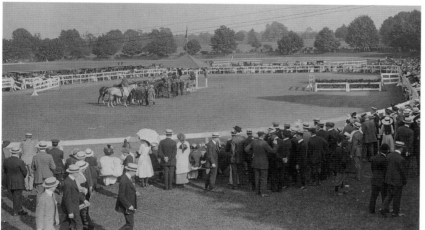

◄ Excluded from earlier shows, the jumper class was added around 1910 when the show returned to the polo grounds.

(Photo courtesy Devon Horse Show and Country Fair, Inc.)

◄ ▼ Entrants from Philadelphia and Pennsylvania State Police squads lined up for competition in 1910.

(Photo courtesy Devon Horse Show and Country Fair, Inc.)

▼ Preparing for the hunt. Fox hunting was a popular sport at the inn. Many hunts were held in conjunction with the Radnor Hunt Club.

*(Photo courtesy
Devon Horse Show and Country Fair, Inc.)*

EXTRACTS OF THE DEVON HORSE SHOW
From The Spur.

The fine equine spectacle at Devon

Once again the Devon Horse Show Association conclusively demonstrated that in quality, number of exhibits and attendance it is the most important outdoor exhibition in the country. There are no side issues, no "attractions"; there is nothing but the horse and the varied classes for four full days of morning and afternoon sessions.

THE SPUR

A heavy rain on the opening day was laughed at, raincoats appeared as if by magic and horse-loving fashionables of the important Main Line and of Philadelphia lined Devon's tree-embowered oval.

Some idea of the heavy classes may be grasped when it is stated that thirty hunters, twenty-five jumpers, eighteen roadsters and eight tandems appeared in various classes—all of superb quality. In the harness classes the return to his best form of Nala, possibly the greatest action horse of his era. But for the accident of "pulling his shoe" when in the middle of his exhibition he would surely have won and he may be safely classed as good as ever. The heavy draft horses were a wonderful display. They

Conshohocken, Pa., October 7th, 1886.

A meeting of the **Gulf Mills Hunt** will be held at **Devon Inn**, *Devon Station*, P. R. R., on Monday, October 11th, 1886, at 8 P. M.

The advisability of a change of Article III of By-Laws, conferring on the Master of the Hounds in place of the President the appointment of the Hunt Committee, will be considered.

A meeting of the Stockholders will be held at the same time and place, to adopt a By-Law governing the ownership and transfer of stock.

HENRY M. TRACY, SEC'Y.

Devon Golf Club

Colors: Red and green

THE DEVON GOLF CLUB enjoys the distinction of a paradox. It has no clubhouse, yet it is housed in one of the most extensive and costly buildings in the country. Indeed, the club, *per se*, is a condition unto itself. Called into life by the first fragment breath of early spring, and flourishing in apparently perennial vigor all summer, it fades and dies away on the first approach of each winter, and is as unlike its kindred organizations who worship at the same athletic shrine, as it very well could be. Yet another distinction is enjoyed by the club. Its nine-hole course was the first mapped out in the neighborhood of Philadelphia, and the first team match ever played around the Quaker City was contested over its links. These facts are more fully dealt with elsewhere, but to such enthusiasts as Mr. Angelo T. Freedley, Mr. Sidney G. Fisher, Mr. Marcellus Coxe, Mr. Montgomery Wilcox and the pres-

LEWIS A. RILEY
President

ent President, Mr. Lewis A. Riley, the club owes its very existence. At the time of writing there was some talk of the links being abandoned owing to the building encroachments in the neighborhood, but golfers, who have enjoyed the sport over its charming distances, sincerely hope the day is far distant when their opportunities for an indulgence in their favorite pastime is curtailed. The links are well laid out, extending as they do over some 40 acres. Some of the bunkers are artificial; others are natural. The course is flanked on all sides by long lush grass, the presence of which has caused the downfall of many an excellent player from courses not so difficult and soul-trying. A drive and a pitch is demanded at nearly every hole, the fifth is a cleek but interest abounds. In looking back to the time when golf was first played over these distances, it is amusing to recall that a card of 100 for the round of nine holes was particularly gratifying to the early membership.

The Links

Total length:—2204 yards.

Par score:—32½, as follows:

3½ 3½ 3½ 3½ 3 4 3½ 4 4

Laid out by:—Marcellus Coxe and Montgomery Wilcox.

How to reach:—Three minutes' walk from Devon Station on

106

the main line of the Pennsylvania Railroad; 17 miles from Philadelphia.

The Club

Annual meeting and election:—In June.

Officers

President:—Lewis A. Riley.
Treasurer:—W. W. Curtin.
Secretary:—Mahlon Hutchinson.
Hotel guests pay an annual charge of $5.

Devon Golf Club

Holes	Distances Yards	Distances and Bogie Bogie
1	228	4
2	248	4
3	223	4
4	234	3
5	182	4
6	304	4
7	239	4
8	265	4
9	281	4
Total	2204	35

THE PIERCE MOTORETTE, STANHOPES AND TOURING CARS, 6¾ H. P. TO 24 H. P.
Banker Brothers Company Automobile Palace, 620, 631, 633 North Broad Street, Philadelphia, Pittsburg and

107

▲ 1903 Golfers Record and photograph
(Courtesy the Historical Society of Pennsylvania)

George Crump, one of the original innkeepers of the Devon Inn, moved to New Jersey in 1900 to follow his hotel business pursuits. Crump did very well in the hotel business and was able to engage himself in other interests, especially golf. In 1913, his love of golf led him to design and build the Pine Valley Golf Course in New Jersey. The construction period took a few years, but in 1918, George Crump died before he saw his course completed.

▶ A map view of Devon's parks in 1900. The developers of Devon promoted the park-like, country setting for their resort's locale.
(Courtesy Franklin Maps, King of Prussia, PA)

▼ A panoramic rear and side view from atop the inn. Sugartown Road is pictured on the left in the background landscape, closest to the horizon. The golf course and some parks belonging to the inn were located in this area of Sugartown Road, which was then called Devon Avenue. The cottages to the right in the background appear along Berkley Road near Waterloo Road.
(Circa early 1900 photo courtesy Radnor Historical Society)

▶ *Golfers photo courtesy The Historical Society of Pennsylvania*

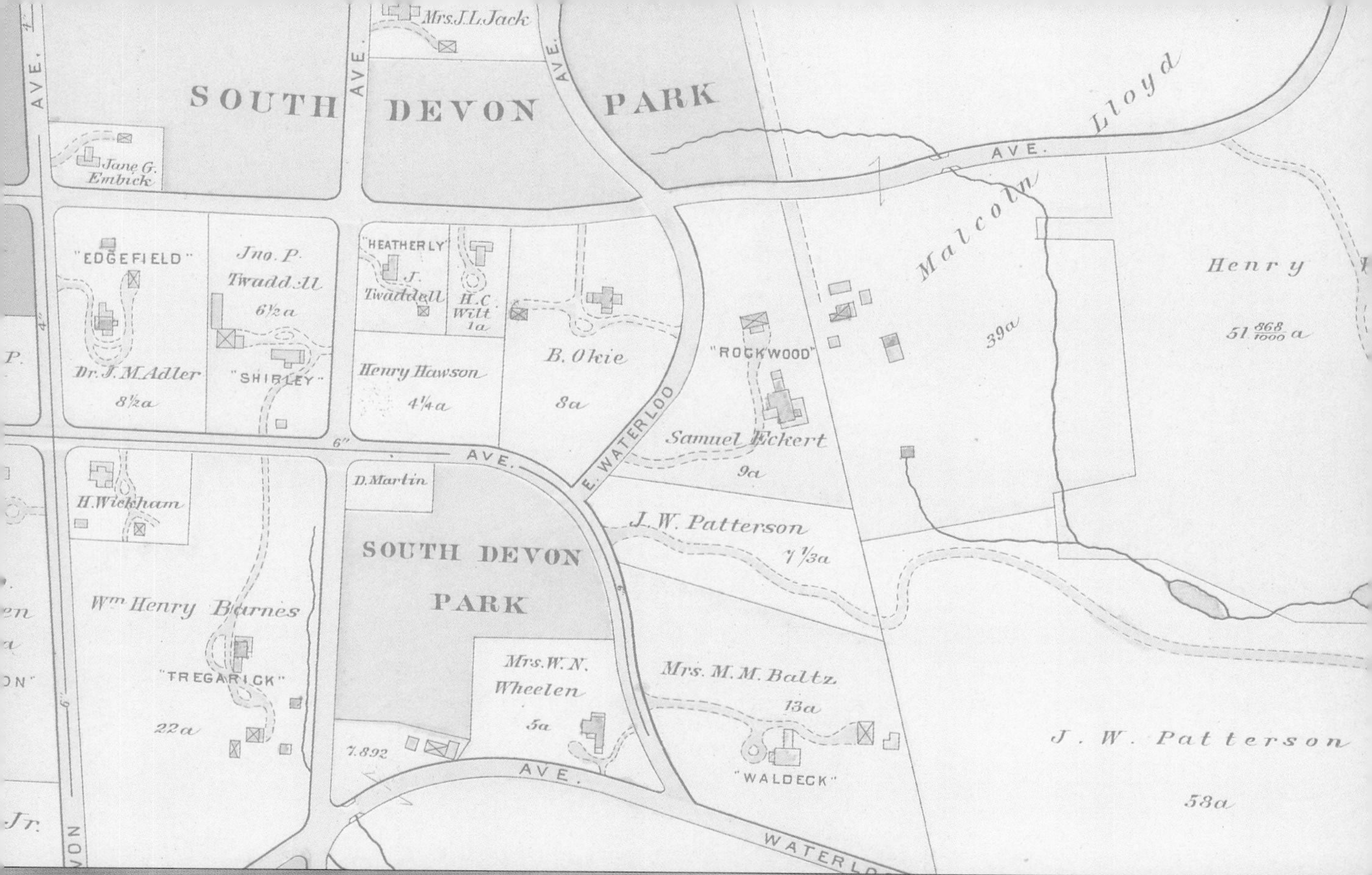

Top map:

SOUTH DEVON PARK

Mrs. J. L. Jack

AVE. AVE.

AVE. Lloyd

Jane G. Embick

"EDGEFIELD" Jno. P. Twadd.ll. 6½a

HEATHERLY J. Twaddell

H. C. Wilt 1a

Malcolm 39a

Henry 51 868/1000 a

Dr. J. M. Adler 8½a "SHIRLEY"

Henry Hawson 4¼a

B. Okie 8a

"ROCKWOOD"

Samuel Eckert 9a

E. WATERLOO

H. Wickham

D. Martin

AVE. 6"

J. W. Patterson 7⅓a

SOUTH DEVON PARK

Wm Henry Barnes "TREGARICK" 22a

Mrs. W. N. Wheelen 5a

Mrs. M. M. Baltz 13a

J. W. Patterson 53a

7.892

"WALDECK"

AVE.

WATERLOO

Jr.

Bottom map:

SOUTH

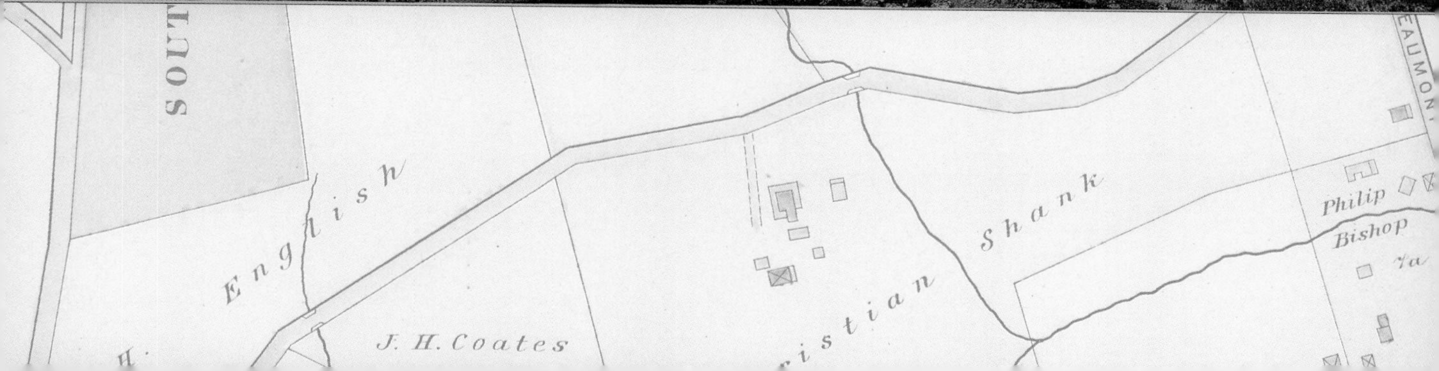

English

Beaumont

Christian Shank

Philip Bishop 7a

J. H. Coates

▲ A 2007 photo of the original section of the Wilbur's hilltop home. Due to its close proximity to the mill and general configuration of the original structure and out buildings, the early home and occupants were most likely associated with the farming industry, dating back to the 1700s.

◀ The Wilburs' wedding invitation.
(Courtesy Toby Charrington)

▶ Around 1895, William N. Wilbur, famous for Wilbur Chocolates, and his wife, Elizabeth Fitch, purchased their hilltop property in Devon. Within a few years, the Wilburs increased their land holdings by purchasing neighboring parcels of land, which included the property that contained the Waterloo Mill. Architectural records seem to indicate that the Wilburs transformed the original farmhouse, which was located on their property, into a grand country manor around 1900 and named it Idlewood Farm.

According to architectural projects secured by the Wilburs between 1895 and 1905, the home's transformation from farmhouse to a country Victorian Tudor seems to reflect the characteristics associated with the architectural design style of R. Brognard Okie, a locally renowned architect at the time. Soon after the home's initial transformation, the exterior's dark wood trim and plaster were painted to the all white exterior that's apparent at this time.

Renamed by another owner, "Hilltop House" is under the stewardship of Easttown Township by the generosity of Dr. and Mrs. Sterg O'Dell. The manor home has been made available for weddings, parties and special events, in the same grand style as the Wilbur Family meant it to be.

(Hilltop House watercolor by Gail Grams, courtesy Easttown Township)

▲ Portraits of William and Elizabeth Wilbur.
(Courtesy Toby Charrington)

◄ With Devon's resort era in full swing, Idlewood Farm gave the Wilburs a unique opportunity to share the home's elegant grandeur by holding galas and events most associated with wealthy individuals and families. The Wilburs continued to entertain until they sold Idlewood in 1919.

(Circa 1907 Radnor Hunt luncheon invitation courtesy Chester County Historical Society)

The history of Wilbur Chocolates dates back to 1865 when William's father, H. O. Wilbur, was a successful hardware and stove merchant in Vineland, New Jersey. The opportunity came along to unite with Samuel Croft, a confectionery merchant in Philadelphia. The two formed Croft & Wilbur, producing molasses and hard candy. The candy was sold to the railroad company for train boys to sell.

By 1884, the business grew to include the manufacture of cocoa and chocolate. H. O. Wilbur & Sons was formed to produce the chocolate products, while Croft continued production of other candy varieties under his own name. In 1887, Wilbur & Sons moved into a larger facility in Philadelphia where the business was so successful that the senior Wilbur was able to retire at age 59, placing the chocolate business in the hands of his sons.

During the early 1890's, William Wilbur brought two brothers, Steve and Mass Oriole, from France to assist in developing other lines of chocolate sundries. In 1894, the Wilbur Bud, designed to resemble a flower bud, was introduced. When Lawrence Wilbur (third generation) returned to the Philadelphia business from studying chocolate manufacturing in Germany, he developed the machine to foil-wrap the Wilbur Buds. The wrapped method was discontinued in the early years.

In 1930, after various mergers and acquisitions throughout the years, Wilbur Chocolates moved their Philadelphia business to Lititz, Pennsylvania. Today, after more than 120 years, you can still enjoy Wilbur Chocolates.

...ke pouring from the top of the Devon Manor gives some idea of the fury of the blaze which swept the convalescent home on Tuesday. Patients were evacuated to Bryn Mawr Hospital and nearby nursing homes without incident, thanks to the efficiency of firemen, ambulance crews, Red Cross volunteers and Manor employees.   Photo by Charles Donnelly

▲ Built around 1885 in Devon, "Llangollen" was the summer home to Dr. Thomas, a leading homeopathic physician of Philadelphia. After spending summers with his family at the Devon Inn, Dr. Thomas eventually purchased the hilltop property when it became available. Later in life when Dr. Thomas was in ill health, he permanently moved to his country estate to live out his final days. Llangollen's ownership changed throughout the years, and in 1967, the stately home was damaged by fire. Llangollen continues its presence on the Devon hilltop, but only hidden by a different façade.

(Newspaper photo courtesy Suburban and Wayne Times)

42

◄ 1930s aerial view of the Llangollen property

▼ ▼ A 2007 view of what is believed to be remaining from the Devon Inn's man-made lake located on Lancaster Avenue in Devon. Records indicate that Dr. Thomas, who was a frequent guest at the inn, stocked the lake with carp when it was built around 1884. The lake, at its full capacity, was used for boating and fishing activities of the guests staying at the inn. In winter ice was cut and stored until the following summer season. For fire protection, the sprinkler system's water was pumped from the lake and stored in the inn's cupola.

► A 2007 view at the intersection of Lancaster Avenue and Sugartown Road; only a portion of the original cluster of attached homes remain today along Lancaster Avenue.

A view of a horse and buggy entering Lancaster Avenue from Old Sugartown Road in the late 1880s.

▲ Lancaster Avenue in the late 1880's.

(Courtesy Radnor Historical Society)

◄ In 1897, "Tregarick" was William H. Barnes' summer home on Exeter Road in Devon. Barnes held many positions within the railway system. To mention a few, Barnes was president of the Allegheny Valley Railway Co., Western New York & Pennsylvania Railway Company, and director of the Pennsylvania Railroad. At one point, the original 200-year-old structure was enlarged. Home is presently a private residence.

(Courtesy Library Company of Philadelphia)

◄ Around 1880, "Edgefield" was a country home to Dr. John M. Adler, a physician from Philadelphia. The home is located on Sugartown Road (then-named Devon Avenue) in Devon and was in existence before the Revolutionary War. In 1883, when the first Devon Inn was destroyed by fire, Dr. Adler provided shelter in his home for some of the guests until they could make other arrangements. Dr. Adler and his family enjoyed the home for a number of years.

▼ "Brendon," located at the corner of Waterloo and Sugartown Roads in Devon, was a summer home to Theodore Kitchen, president of the Central National Bank of Philadelphia in the 1880s. Home is a private residence.

(Circa 1882 photo courtesy Library Company of Philadelphia)

▲ In 1892, Jane G. Embick, daughter of Dr. John M. Adler, of Philadelphia, was one of the first to build a home on a parcel of land within one of Devon's parks. Located at the corner of Sugartown and Dorset Roads, Embick's summer cottage neighbored her father's.

► Around 1900, "Clovelly" in Devon was the summer home of Henry Whelen, Jr. Whelen was a retired naval officer and head of the banking house of Townsend Whelen & Co.

(Photo courtesy Library Company of Philadelphia)

▼ Circa 1902 view of "Fairlawn," located at the corner of Fairfield and Sugartown Roads in Devon. Summer home to architect, John T. Windrim. Windrim was president of the Devon Horse Show in 1910, when the event returned to the Devon Polo Grounds, the same location as today's show.

(Photo courtesy Library Company of Philadelphia)

DEVON HORSE SHOW
Devon, Penna, May 27, 28, 29, 30, 1914
Largest Out-Door Horse Show Ever Held Anywhere

▼ In 1903, Elizabeth J. Shreve, wife of Benjamin Shreve, purchased one of the first parcels of land, which was located on the resort's golf course. The Shreves built their country home around 1905 on Devon Avenue, currently known as Sugartown Road. The 1910 census records indicated that Benjamin was an attorney, and his source of income was recorded as "own income." The census also verified that the Shreves had one servant while in Devon.

Okie

Locally renowned architect of the 1900s, R. Brognard Okie resided at his Hillside Farm Estate in an early circa 1700s home, which he later restored. He was commissioned to recreate William Penn's Estate, Penn's Manor; redesign Philadelphia's Market (High) Street, for the Sesquicentennial Exposition, in 1926; restore the Betsy Ross House in Philadelphia; and developed numerous projects that characterized his popularity as a fine architect. His former estate is located in an area that was once considered Devon and is currently a private residence.

HILLSIDE FARM

PEBBLE SPRING DR.

OTHER USES FOR THE OLD INN

AFTER years of vacancies and unsuccessful transactions, the old Devon Inn was sold in 1919 to the Devon Manor Corporation. In 1920, the building reopened as the Devon Manor, a boarding school for girls. Former President William Howard Taft spoke at the opening ceremonies. In 1924 the school entered into bankruptcy, and the building became vacant once again.

DEVON MANOR

The Beautiful Impressive Approach to the Grounds

Training the American Girl

A SUBURBAN school 16 miles from Philadelphia, Devon Manor enjoys the cultural advantages of that city while commanding the finest surroundings for quiet nerves and concentration of interests. Here the American girl is trained to achieve big, practical things in her future home and civic life. The curriculum is exceptional in the range of subjects beyond the usual college-preparatory and junior-college courses, such as Social Service, Secretaryship, Household Arts and Sciences, Journalism, Music, Art, Arts and Crafts, Expression, Kindergarten. College trained faculty.

Five buildings, sixteen acres for outdoor sports, Tennis, basketball, riding, fencing, hockey, skating, golf. Outdoor class-rooms. School farm. Resident physician, nurse, dietitian. For Booklet, address

Out for a Canter

DEVON MANOR
Box 597
Devon, Pennsylvania
Francis R. Lowell, A.B., President
Edith Samson, Principal

DEVON MANOR

Training Girls for Tomorrow

Devon Manor, anticipating the new and wider demands on the woman of tomorrow, trains a girl to assume with ease her larger rôle within and without the home. Its equipment is complete. Situated sixteen miles from Philadelphia, it enjoys the cultural advantages of that city, while commanding the finest possible country surroundings that make for quiet nerves and concentration of interests.

College-trained faculty. In addition to the usual college preparatory and Junior College courses, training is offered in Social Service, Secretaryship, Household Arts and Sciences, Journalism, Music, Art, Expression, Kindergarten.

Five buildings, sixteen acres. Outdoor classrooms. All outdoor sports. School farm to supply fresh vegetables. Resident physician, nurse and dietitian. The catalog describes the details. Address

DEVON MANOR
Box 887   Devon, Pennsylvania
FRANCIS R. LOWELL, A. B., President
EDITH SAMSON, Principal

▼ The objective of the school's curriculum was to provide a thorough and systematic education for girls, believing that teachers of the future must be directors of human lives, instead of mere purveyors of knowledge. Teachers employed at the school came from Bryn Mawr College, Philadelphia School of Design, Universities of Pennsylvania, Columbia, Drexel and Syracuse, and the chaplain and instructor of sacred studies was the rector from nearby Old Saint Davids Church.

(Photos courtesy Radnor Historical Society)

▲ Circa 1920 view from atop the school.
Lancaster Avenue runs horizontally
in the background.

*(Photo courtesy Radnor Historical Society,
Ad courtesy Lower Merion Historical Society)*

◄ An extensive program in physical training and outdoor life was a top priority. The school featured a hockey field, tennis and basketball courts, golf link privileges, horseback riding, ice-skating in winter, and any other winter sport suitable for girls. In addition to school athletics, courses in physiology, hygiene and gymnastics were included as well. Indoor floor exercises promoting correct posture and better breathing was a must, but whenever possible, outdoor training was preferred.

(Photos courtesy Radnor Historical Society)

◀ Lighting fixtures, carpet patterns, and other interior decorations, carried over from the former inn, can be seen in a photo of a girl's bedroom.

▼ The dining facility used fine linens, china, and silverware from the former inn. Meals were so bountiful at the manor that girls were discouraged from taking food to their rooms. Students were required to pay 25 cents for any meal that wasn't eaten in the dining room.

(Photos courtesy Radnor Historical Society)

Meals were so bountiful at the manor that girls were discouraged from taking food to their rooms. Students were required to pay 25 cents for any meal that wasn't eaten in the dining room.

DEVON DAYS

▶ The school's strong academic course offering included English, math, science, history, physical education, music, bible studies, and other minor subjects, but also an emphasis was placed particularly on diction and the dramatic arts. The school felt that diction and the dramatic arts developed the natural poise, initiative and interpretative abilities of the girls. Clear speaking, combined with spontaneity in gesture and inflection, was considered highly desirable. The time-worn legacy of dramatic performances in the ballroom at the former inn was reborn by the girls at Devon Manor.

▶ The art studio had once provided a multi-room accommodation for the elite clientele staying at the former Devon Inn.

▼ ▶ Domestic science included lessons in cooking and sewing, as well as caring for the home with emphasis on furnishings, ventilation and sanitation. Household physics and chemistry were considered advanced subjects. A bedroom suite from the former inn converted just fine into the school's teaching kitchen.

(Photos courtesy Radnor Historical Society)

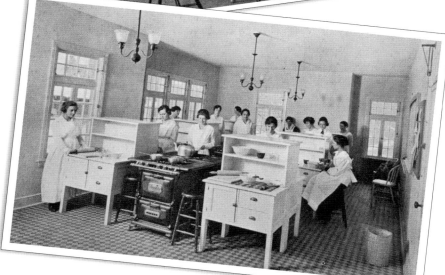

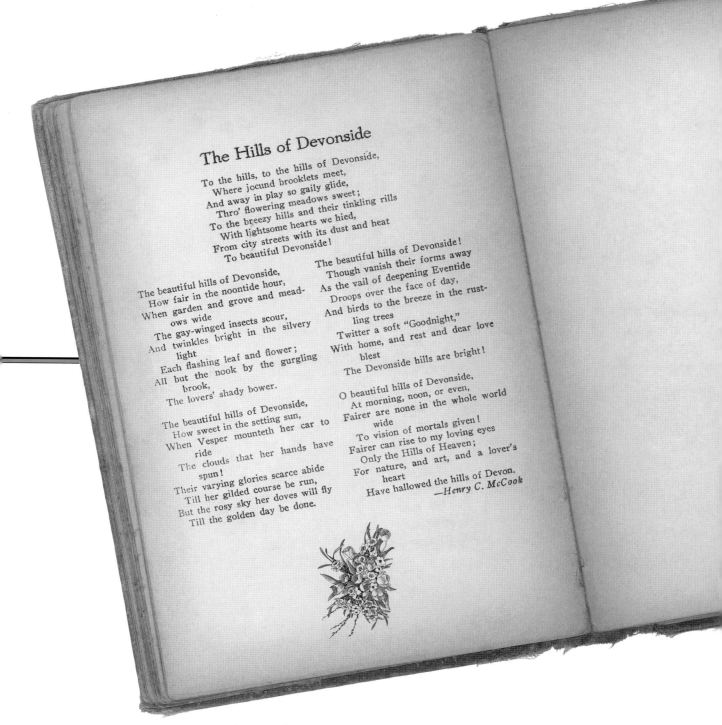

The Hills of Devonside

To the hills, to the hills of Devonside,
Where jocund brooklets meet,
And away in play so gaily glide,
Thro' flowering meadows sweet;
To the breezy hills and their tinkling rills
With lightsome hearts we hied,
From city streets with its dust and heat
To beautiful Devonside!

The beautiful hills of Devonside,
How fair in the noontide hour,
When garden and grove and mead-
ows wide
The gay-winged insects scour,
And twinkles bright in the silvery
light
Each flashing leaf and flower;
All but the nook by the gurgling
brook,
The lovers' shady bower.

The beautiful hills of Devonside,
How sweet in the setting sun,
When Vesper mounteth her car to
ride
The clouds that her hands have
spun!
Their varying glories scarce abide
Till her gilded course be run,
But the rosy sky her doves will fly
Till the golden day be done.

The beautiful hills of Devonside!
Though vanish their forms away
As the vail of deepening Eventide
Droops over the face of day,
And birds to the breeze in the rust-
ling trees
Twitter a soft "Goodnight,"
With home, and rest and dear love
blest
The Devonside hills are bright!

O beautiful hills of Devonside,
At morning, noon, or even,
Fairer are none in the whole world
wide
To vision of mortals given!
Fairer can rise to my loving eyes
Only the Hills of Heaven;
For nature, and art, and a lover's
heart
Have hallowed the hills of Devon.
—*Henry C. McCook*

Devonside Poem

Henry Christopher McCook was an American Presbyterian clergyman, naturalist, and author on religion, history, and nature. Born in New Lisbon, Ohio, in 1837, McCook learned the printing trade as a youth and later attended Jefferson College. His study and observations with nature led him to publish a series of journals, books, and children's books, using illustrations drawn by Daniel Carter Beard, the founder of the Boy Scouts of America. In 1869, he became pastor of the Seventh Presbyterian church of Philadelphia, where he lived until his death. In 1895, McCook designed the official flag of the city of Philadelphia.

(Hills of Devonside, courtesy Radnor Historical Society)

▶ Aerial view of the Devon Park Hotel and Devon Horse Show in progress around 1926.

(Photo courtesy Devon Horse Show and Country Fair, Inc.)

In 1926, the Devon Park Hotel Realty Corporation acquired the former inn property from the girls school, and reopened the building as The Devon Park Hotel. Even though the era of the "roaring twenties" was in full swing, the hotel enjoyed success as the center of Main Line society for only two years.

(Advertisements courtesy Lower Merion Historical Society))

DEVON PARK HOTEL
DEVON, PA.
"KNOWN FOR ITS COMFORT AND GOOD FOOD"

Appealing to discriminating persons for Private Entertaining, Dances, Bridge Parties, Dinners, Banquets, Wedding Receptions and Entertainments.

Catering to Permanent and Transient Guests.

Dancing Every Saturday Evening.

Commencing May 15th. Dancing Every Evening in French Terrace Garden.

Wayne 1350   LINCOLN HIGHWAY

A new school... for boys

Three and one-half miles from Valley Forge, America's great shrine of Revolutionary interest, a new military school for boys has been established. On its ample campus, not far from Philadelphia, an engagement was fought by Light Horse Harry Lee. Nearby is the birthplace of General Anthony Wayne.

The main building cost approximately three-quarters of a million dollars. It has 151 rooms with baths—single baths. The kitchen and bakery are the most fully equipped of any school in the eastern part of the U. S. Recreation building bowling alleys, billiard room. Large auditorium.

Gym under construction. 4½ acres for outdoor drill and recreation. Polo, golf. Cavalry unit. College Entrance Board Requirements are the scholastic standard. The aim is to bring out the best in each individual—to teach boys how to study and to give them thorough preparation for college or business. Classical, scientific, commercial courses.

The school has a 200-foot elevation on the Lincoln Highway, in a "safe line" suburb of Philadelphia. Undenominational—Christian influence. Write for catalog.

The Commandant, Devon, Pa.

Valley Forge Military Academy

▼ Removing most of the bedroom's former luxurious identity, the academy's remodeling efforts maintained only the basic accommodations that suited the students' needs. Bedrooms equipped with private or semi-private baths from the old inn days, were reserved for faculty and staff only.

(Photo courtesy Radnor Historical Society)

▶ The Devon Park Hotel Realty Corporation reorganized in 1928, and with Captain Milton Baker, the organization became known as the Valley Forge Military Academy Realty Corporation. After some remodeling, the building opened as the original school to the Valley Forge Military Academy with Captain Baker as the superintendent, a staff of thirteen, and 117 cadets.

(Circa 1928 photo courtesy The Historical Society of Pennsylvania)

◀ ◀ The academy's faculty was known to be one of the strongest along the East Coast at that time. A majority of the original class of cadets were from Pennsylvania and New Jersey and a few from Massachusetts, New York, Michigan, and Virginia. The class schedule consisted of five one-hour periods per day with a two-hour evening study session, five days per week. The students were required to participate in at least one sport activity each day during the school year.

(Photo courtesy Radnor Historical Society)

◀ An assembly of cadets pictured just days before the devastating fire destroyed the school.

(Photo courtesy Radnor Historical Society)

▼ The academy spent time in Devon for only a few months. On January 18, 1929, a disastrous fire destroyed the former inn once again. At the time, there was some speculation that the academy would rebuild on the same site. But in July of that same year, the decision was made to purchase the 27-acre former St. Luke's School site (present site of academy) and build fireproof brick barracks of a Colonial design.

(Fire photos courtesy Radnor Historical Society)

EARLY LIFE AROUND ÐEVON

THE Gamble House was considered to be one of the first structures built around 1801 on Old Lancaster Road in a small community, then known as Glassley Commons. Philadelphia merchant Robert McClenachan planned the commons around 1800 in an area that is now considered Devon. Glassley was intended to be a flourishing town with streets, avenues and alleys, designed to reflect the block layout pattern of a city such as Philadelphia. The plan included a school, tavern, and the perfect street layout, but without any industries to attract residents, the town's existence surrendered to failure. The Gamble House was demolished in the mid 1800s.

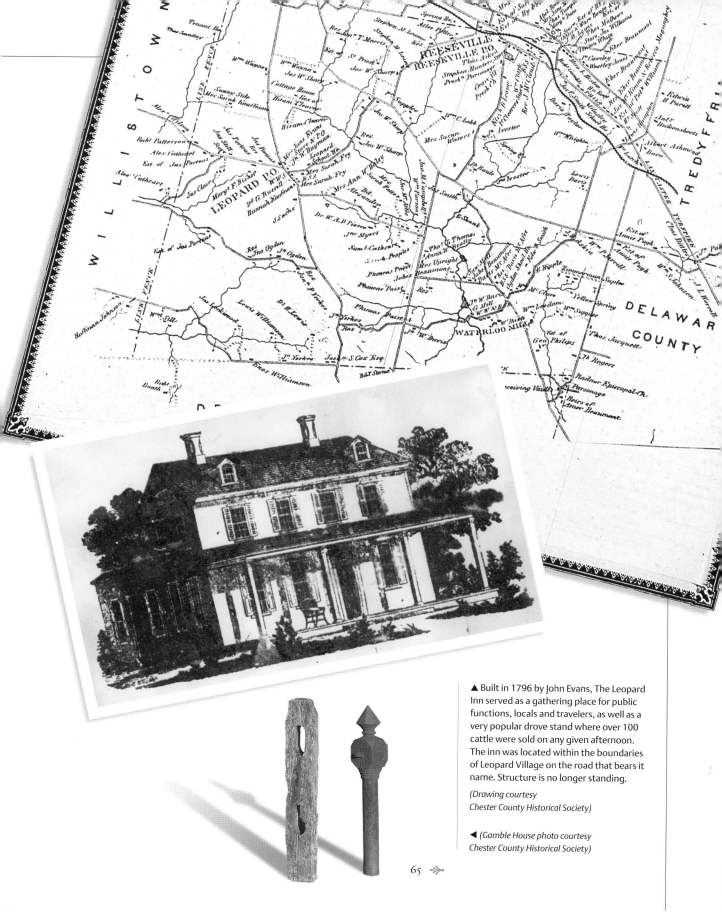

▲ Built in 1796 by John Evans, The Leopard Inn served as a gathering place for public functions, locals and travelers, as well as a very popular drove stand where over 100 cattle were sold on any given afternoon. The inn was located within the boundaries of Leopard Village on the road that bears it name. Structure is no longer standing.

(Drawing courtesy Chester County Historical Society)

◀ *(Gamble House photo courtesy Chester County Historical Society)*

▼ Dr. and Mrs. Eldon Graham purchased "Eldonridge" around 1905. Located on a Devon hilltop, this home was the Graham's country estate. The only available history on the property is that it was originally used as an inn that dated back to the Revolution. The home has since been converted into apartment units.

(Circa 1916 photo courtesy Chester County Historical Society)

▶ A 1916 view of the grounds in front of "Eldonridge."

(Courtesy Chester County Historical Society)

The hamlet of Waterloo Mills sits along Waterloo Road in Devon, where the road crosses over Darby Creek. From 1798 through the early 1900s, Waterloo Mills was significant for its association with the milling industry, crop and dairy farming, and as an ice production venue in the late 1800s. By 1810, Chester County became known as the "beef fattening capital of the world" and produced more cheese than any other Pennsylvania county. The mill's close proximity to Conestoga Road made it an ideal location to transport goods to Philadelphia.

In 1793, Mordecai Davis purchased the Davis/Gallagher Farm, which was originally, part of the land patented to William Wood from William Penn in 1684. After Mordecai's death, his son, John W. Davis, continued his father's legacy of farming and enlarging the property. Through a sheriff's sale in 1850, Davis purchased the 60-acre parcel of land that contained the mill.

In 1877, the Davis' property experienced a subdivision, allowing Allison Alexander to purchase the 30-acre tract that contained the mill. Facing stiff competition with the western flour milling industry, Alexander refitted the mill with improved rollers and continued to mill into the 20th Century. The mill property was sold when wealthy Philadelphians purchased land for country estate homebuilding, thus ending the once profitable industry of this Chester County community.

(2007 Photo by Peter DePiano, Jr.)

◄ The historic context of Waterloo Mills no longer exists today, but the buildings and their original architectural characters have changed very little. Many structures within the mill area are privately owned.

In 1995, Waterloo Mills was placed on the National Register of Historic Places and is preserved by the Brandywine Conservancy as a historic area for many years to come. The Waterloo Mills Historic District offers us a small glimpse into the every-day life of our early settlers.

(Photo from the Dorothy Reed Collection, courtesy Herb Fry))

◄ Mordecai Davis developed his land holdings by building a springhouse, barn, and black-smith/wheelwright shop. Circa 1800s view shows the blacksmith and wheelwright shop in disrepair. The shop has since been recon-structed into a two- story garage opposite the mill on Waterloo Road.

(Photo courtesy Radnor Historical Society)

▼ Happy Creek Farm, situated along Church Road in Devon, is a peaceful reminder of a time long ago. In 1748, Humphrey Wayne purchased 150 acres of the original Harrison tract located within the area. Over the years, the property transferred among members of the Wayne family, including Anthony Wayne, and remained in the family until 1790.

Around 1805, when nearby Waterloo Mills was a thriving industry, Mordecai Davis, then proprietor of the milling venue, purchased the above tract of land which included the cottage at right to increase his holdings for additional farmland and tenant farmhouses for his workers. The farmhouse and barn were built following his purchase. The tract of land has been subdivided over the years since Davis was owner, and presently, the farmhouse and cottage remain as private residences.

(Photo by Peter DePiano, Jr.)

▼ During the time the Wayne family had ownership of the 150-acre tract, records seem to indicate that an uncle built the cottage on a portion of the property for Hannah Wayne as a wedding gift.

HAPPY CREEK
— FARM —

Phillips – Harrison
House

circa 1830

▼ Chesterbrook, originally recognized as a farming community, dates back to the 1700s. During the Revolutionary War, Generals Charles Lee and Thomas Bradford occupied the main farmhouse as their headquarters. The farmhouse is often referred to as the Lee-Bradford House.

Alexander J. Cassatt, railroad mogul and brother of well-known painter, Mary Cassatt, purchased Chesterbrook around 1881 as a gentleman's country farm to breed thoroughbred racehorses. His close friend and well-established architect, Frank Furness, of Furness, Evans & Co., designed the farm's main barn.

Cassatt's training abilities with horses led him to be the recipient of many competition wins. His horses won the 1886 Preakness Stakes with The Bard; 1889 Belmont Stakes with horse Eric; 1890 Preakness with Montague; and the 1891 Belmont with Foxford. In 1895, Cassatt assisted in organizing the National Steeplechase Association for steeplechase horseracing. Cassatt also introduced the United States to the Hackney pony, and along with other horse enthusiasts, founded the American Hackney Horse Society that continues today in Lexington Kentucky.

Alexander J. Cassatt died in 1906 of whooping cough. The legacy of a gentleman's horse farm faded away following Cassatt's death, but the farm remained in the family and continued its existence by producing prize-winning milk from their Guernsey cows.

(Circa 1900 view of barns and outbuildings courtesy Anne Boland. Anne's father-in-law, Peter J. Boland, was at one time, manager of the Chesterbrook Farm)

◀ A 2007 view of a restyled barn that at one time belonged to Alexander J. Cassatt. The former barn is presently an academy for children.

IN UNMARKED GRAVES
WITHIN THIS ANCIENT BURIAL GROUND
WERE LAID THE BODIES OF MANY SOLDIERS
OF THE AMERICAN REVOLUTION
WHOSE NAMES SO FAR AS KNOWN
ARE INSCRIBED UPON THIS BOULDER.
IN GRATEFUL REMEMBRANCE OF
THE COMMON DEBT DUE THESE HUMBLE PATRIOTS
THIS MEMORIAL
WAS DEDICATED ANNO DOMINI MCMV ON THE
ONE HUNDRED AND TWENTY-NINTH ANNIVERSARY
OF THE DECLARATION OF INDEPENDENCE.

▶ Located on Irish Road in Berwyn, Cockleburr Cabin was built around 1710 during the time Berwyn was called Cockletown. Throughout the years, owners have discovered many ancient American Indian relics on the property. Located within feet of one of the oldest Indian trails along Conestoga Road, Cockleburr surely shared its existence with the Delaware and Lenape Indians.

One of the first known pre-revolutionary inhabitants of Cockleburr was Whitehead Wetherby until he sold the property in 1772. Whitehead was the son of Benjamin Wetherby who was brother-in-law to Dr. Bernhardus Van Leer, one-time innkeeper of the old Blue Ball Inn on Conestoga Road. Historical accounts show that the Wetherbys moved when Whitehead's wife, Hannah, inherited Grove Hall (Travelgwyn) on Waterloo Avenue when her mother Ann James died in 1773. Whitehead Wetherby was Easttown's first Justice of the Peace in 1800.

Many families occupied the cabin since the Wetherbys, including Conrad Wilson, former president of the Chester County Historical Society and the Tredyffrin/Easttown History Club. When Conrad was a young boy living in the area, he made a sketch of the cabin and carried it in his wallet wishing that someday he would be able to purchase the cabin. His wish came true and Conrad and his family resided in the cabin from about 1952 through 1967.

On April 2, 1973, Cockleburr was placed on the National Register of Historic Places and is a true reminder of days gone by.

(Photo by Peter DePiano, Jr.)

The Old Eagle School Cemetary

Extracted from The Old Eagle School, Tredyffrin, by Shannon Keller

Where 'neath the sod, within the sacred lea,
Rests many a soldier, too, in dreamless sleep,
Who freely offered life that Liberty
Might yield the fruit posterity should reap.

Here when their part in life was bravely one
Their tired bodies found a Mother's breast.
Untroubled now by battles lost or won,
They consecrate the ground to peace and rest

◄ Sometime after Conrad Wilson purchased Cockleburr, he moved a former schoolroom structure from the Daylesford train station and old Blue Ball Inn area to his property to be used as a garden shed. The schoolroom was at one time Daylesford's only school after the Mt. Airy School was demolished in 1895. Agnes Okie taught at the schoolroom for about five years sometime around 1915-1920.

Before the vacant schoolroom was moved, it was used during 1930s -1950s as a clubhouse and library reading room for the Tredyffrin/Easttown History Club. Initially, the club had to pay a one-dollar rental fee to the Croasdales, then owners of the old Blue Ball Inn until the structure was donated to the history club. After a series of break-ins and vandalism, the use of the clubhouse was discontinued.

The schoolroom garden shed never had an official name, but when Mildred Erdman acquired the Cockleburr property, she named the former schoolroom, The Daylesford University. Even though the sign has weathered over the years, it continues to swing today.

(Photo by Peter DePiano, Jr.)

▲ Built in 1705, on land belonging to William Penn's daughter, Letitia Penn, The Camp School is believed to be one of the oldest one-room schoolhouses in the area. The school site is located in Valley Forge National Park and is mentioned in many historical publications as a school dating back to the early 1700s. It was used by the Continental Army as a hospital during the winter of 1777–78.

(Photo by Peter DePiano, Jr.)

▶ Howellville Elementary School was located along Swedesford Road in Howellville. In 1906, the third annual school reunion brought together former teachers and students with their families. The school was destroyed by fire in 1923.

(Reunion invitation and photos courtesy Stephen DiAddezio)

▶ Built as a log structure around 1767, The Old Eagle School in Strafford was used as a school during the week and a church on Sundays. In 1788, the log schoolhouse was replaced with a stone structure on the same site. The tuition fee was two dollars per school term quarter, or three cents per day. Students provided their own goose quill pens and made ink by soaking rusty nails in water. The schoolroom was divided with girls on one side and boys on the other. Around 1836, the school became part of the public school system and continued to serve the children in area until it closed around 1900.

(Circa late 1800s photo courtesy Radnor Historical Society)

Diamond Rock School 1880s

2007

Old Eagle School in 2007

▲ ◄ The Diamond Rock School, an octagonal schoolhouse, opened in 1818 as one of the first public schools in Southeastern, PA. Under a 999-year lease, George Beaver donated the land on which the school was built. The school cost $260.93 to build, and the first schoolmaster was James Mowe. Wharton Esherick, local wood sculpturer, used the school after it closed as his studio from 1915–1919.

(1880s Diamond Rock School photo courtesy Margaret DePiano)

▶ Henry Ruth, a weaver by trade, purchased the Fox Tavern property in 1784. Ruth tried to obtain a tavern license in 1786 by pleading his case that there were no public houses within a ten-mile radius of his property, and that many travelers stop by his place requesting water to drink. The petition was denied until later when he reapplied under the designation of innkeeper. In 1793, he sold the Fox property to Jacob Waters, a blacksmith from Upper Merion.

The property transferred many times since 1793, but records indicate that the Fox remained a tavern or inn until the early 1800s. Around 1808, the property was sold to John Smith, a grocer from Philadelphia. The appearance of the Fox has changed much since its days of welcoming travelers along the old Lancaster Turnpike.

(Photo by Marc Heppe)

The Spread Eagle Tavern and Inn was built in 1796 in the village of Eagle, presently known as Strafford. Eagle had the only relay station west of Philadelphia, making it an important mail and travel stop for Conestoga wagons transporting goods along the Lancaster Turnpike (Old Lancaster Road) from the city.

In 1798, during Philadelphia's yellow fever epidemic, the inn was used for members of Congress and ambassadors from foreign countries. By 1884, wagon trains gave way to the locomotive and the once busy inn began its decline.

The inn was sold in 1884 to George W. Childs of Philadelphia. Childs later donated the old inn to the Lincoln Institution of Philadelphia to be used as a summer residence for Indian girls who attended the institute. Several Indian tribes visited the school during the two summers the girls were in residence. Sitting Bull, the celebrated Indian chief and Sioux leader who defeated General George Custer at the Battle of Little Bighorn in 1876, was known to visit frequently. Sitting Bull and his wife brought provisions to the Indian girls when they visited their niece.

(Circa 1886 photos courtesy Radnor Historical Society)

▼ In the early 1700s the village of Howellville was an ideal location for sawmills and gristmills powered by the waters of Crabby Creek. Howell's tavern, or inn, was a popular watering hole and lodging establishment for early travelers.

In 1771, Anthony Wayne and two of his closest friends, Caleh Jones and Jacob Malin, were involved in an incident at the Howell. Apparently, Jacob Malin's wife went over to the Howell to retrieve her less-than-sober husband, when a drunken tavern girl, who considered Mrs. Malin an unwelcome form of competition, tackled her. An all out brawl occurred when master Malin tried to pull apart the fighting wildcats. Wayne and Jones stepped in and tried unsuccessfully to separate the combatants. All were eventually held in bail until emotions were at a more peaceful level.

Cannonball bocce was a popular game to play on the tavern grounds. There were no scores to tally, but the only rule was that the person who rolled the ball the shortest distance, had to carry the others back to the starting line.

In 1777, Sir Charles Gray, the British major general, nicknamed "Cold Steel" Gray, held the "Howell" as his headquarters. Gray acquired the nickname after the Paoli Massacre, because he ordered his men to remove the flints from their muskets and surprise the Americans with a bayonet attack.

(Circa 1934, Howellville Inn photo courtesy the Paoli Library, Frances H. Ligget Collection)

Valley Forge

Valley Forge received its name from the iron forge built along Valley Creek in the 1740s. By the time of the Revolution, a sawmill and gristmill had been added, making the place an important supply base for the Americans. The British destroyed the forge and mills in 1777, and only ruins remained at the time of the encampment.

The women present at Valley Forge included hundreds of enlisted men's wives who followed the army year round, and some general officers' wives on extended visits. The army compensated full-time women followers for rendering such valuable services as sewing, laundering, and nursing.

Hardship did occur at Valley Forge, but the encampment experience could be characterized as "suffering as usual," for privation was the Continental soldier's constant companion. The reason many Americans picture Valley Forge as the pinnacle of misery is that this early and romanticized version of the encampment story became a convenient parable to teach us about American perseverance. Unfortunately, the caricature of starving troops has kept us from getting to know the men of the Continental Army—who they were, why they joined the army, and what they actually accomplished at Valley Forge.

(Extracted from a Valley Forge brochure, courtesy the National Parks Service, Valley Forge, PA, Photos and postcards courtesy Margaret DePiano)

▲ ▶Valley Creek Road circa 1880s.

▶ Washington's Headquarters 1906.

◄ Founded by the John Kennedy family, in the early 1800s, Port Kennedy, an industrial village in Valley Forge, was known for manufacturing lime. The industry's growth was supported by being located near the Philadelphia and Reading Railroad, which supplied a faster mode of transporting lime to Philadelphia.

John Kennedy built his home high on a hilltop in 1852, where he could have a bird's eye view of his manufacturing business. The home transitioned into a restaurant back in the late 1890s, and continued as one under different ownerships for many years.

BUSINESS, COMMERCE, PEOPLE AND PLACES

THE generations of Devonites, mostly Italian and Irish immigrants, used their heritage of a strong work ethic and family unity to get them through the economic hardships of a depressed economy. During the 1930s and beyond, Devon began to prosper once again with businesses and industries moving into its community.

▲ G. B. Wheeler advertisement and photo of Devon home.

(Courtesy Lower Merion Historical Society)

(Billheads courtesy Stephen DiAddezio)

▼ Established in the early 1900s, C.A. Lobb and Sons, was a supplier of lumber, coal, stone, cement, corn and other farm and dairy items. Lobb's followed the Pratts animal and poultry regulations in place at the time, and offered ointments, remedies, and even some cures for animal ailments. Their Devon location along the railroad at Old Lancanster Road and Lancaster Avenue, provided a beneficial spot for receiving and transporting goods.

(Courtesy Radnor Historical Society)

| BUFF & MARY'S HOUSE | TAYLOR GIFTS | CURRY TRAVEL |

▶ Following the Lobb and Sons operation at Old Lancaster Road and Lancaster Avenue, the site became an industrious location for Devon Building Supply and Spinelli Brothers for many years. All but a glimpse of the former structure at this corner location is standing.

(Photo courtesy Herb Fry)

▶ Photo of the coal chute at Spinelli Brothers.

(Photo courtesy Dan DiAddezio and the late Joe Spinelli)

Aerial photo of Devon Building Supply.

(Courtesy Dan DiAddezio and the late Martin Spinelli)

MARTINI'S
RESTAURANT
WAYNE 9744

ITALIAN SPAGHETTI
CHOICE LIQUORS, WINES, ETC.

LINCOLN HIGHWAY
DEVON, PA.

ORIGINAL MARTINI HOUSE & GROCERY STORE   MARTINI'S BAR & RESTAURANT

PLEAS...   Sort?...

Hamburger
Cheeseburger
Liverwurst
Bacon, Lettuc
Pepper & Egg
Provolone Chee
Club
Tuna Salad
Grilled Cheese
Ham & Cheese

Tomato Juice
Soup du Jour
Shrimp Cocktail
Provolone, Pimentos and A
Anchovies, Pimentos and Tom
Antipasto

Breaded Veal Cutlet
Veal Scallopini, Tom
Veal Scallopini, Mars
Roast Sirloin of Beef
Broiled Pork Chops
Fried Filet of Flounder
Grilled Chopped Sirloin
Combination Seafood
Broiled Sirloin Steak
Fried Chicken
Roasted Chicken
Breaded Chicken a la Parm

Our Spec...

Baked Lasagna   6.00
Baked Manicotti   6.50
Home Made Cheese Ravioli & Meatballs   6.00
Home Made Cheese Ravioli & Meatsauce   6.00
Home Made Cheese Ravioli & Mushrooms   6.50
Spaghetti and Tomato Sauce   6.50
Spaghetti and Meatballs   7.00
Spaghetti and Mushrooms   6.50
Spaghetti and Chicken Livers   6.50
Spaghetti, Meatsauce and Mushrooms
Spaghetti Marinara
Spaghetti Aglio y Olio (IOU)
Spaghetti, Clam Sauce (red or white)
Combination Spaghetti and Ravioli with Meatballs
Combination Spaghetti, Ravioli and Rigatoni and Meatballs
Rigatoni and Meatballs
Spaghetti and Sausage   1.50
Potato Gnocchi with Meatballs   1.50

Ita

Garlic Bread 1.75

Desserts

Bisque Tortoni   1.50   Spumoni
Pie   1.50   Ice Cream

Coffee - Tea 1.00 Sanka 1.00 Milk 1.00 Soft Drinks 1.00

By the bottle:

Ruffino
Bolla Valpolicella
Soave Bolla
Elmo Pio
Mateus
Champagne (bottle/split)
Mumms, Great Western

Exqui...

MARTI...

RE...
A...

LANCASTER AVE.   DE...

▲ Martini's in the 1930s and photo
of DiMartini family.

(Courtesy Mary Ann DiMartini)

BENJAMIN C. BETNER COMPANY

Manufacturers of High Grade Paper Products

LINCOLN HIGHWAY—DEVON

▲ ▶ The Benjamin C. Betner Company was established in Devon around 1927. Despite the "Crash" in 1929 and the Depression of the 1930s, Betner's business experienced steady growth. The company was known to make Maxwell House and Eight O'Clock coffee bags, and in the 1940s, designed and produced the filter bag for the Electrolux vacuum.

Located within a quarter mile of the fireworks factory, Betner's received substantial damage from the fireworks explosion in 1930. Over 1700 panes of glass were shattered, and newly installed steel sashes were blown out. About 40 employees were injured from the blast.

Due to increased demands in 1939, Betner's #2 plant opened nearby to accommodate machines to produce flour bags. The #2 plant was sold in 1943 to the Kalamazoo Vegetable Parchment Company.

In 1953, the Benjamin C. Betner Company merged with the Continental Can Company, producer of paper packaging products. Benjamin C. Betner, Jr., served as the executive vice president of the new company until his retirement. The company continued in Devon under the Continental Can name until 1963, when the plant moved its operation to the old Paoli Industrial Park.

(Circa 1928 Betner's advertisement courtesy Lower Merion Historical Society)

(Continental Can photo courtesy Ernest C. Eadeh, Eadeh Enterprises)

Continental Can Company

◀ Founded around 1909 in Michigan, the Kalamazoo Vegetable Parchment Company (KVP) manufactured parchment paper for food storage. Around 1944, the company moved its Philadelphia plant to Devon on the former #2 Betner Paper property alongside the Pennsylvania Railroad. KVP employed many of the locals from Devon and the surrounding areas to produce their high quality papers. Water used in the paper production was taken from an artesian well located nearby. The Devon plant was an ideal location for receiving raw papermaking products as well as shipping the final product anywhere in the United States. The plant was in operation for more than 20 years.

(Photos courtesy Pat Antrilli)

▼ Site of the former Kalamazoo Vegetable Parchment Paper Co. and the #2 Betner paper bag plant.

(Photo by Peter DePiano, Jr.)

Catcart Home Devon, Pa.

▶ The Eliza Cathcart Home was built in 1893 on Valley Forge Road, in Devon by a trust fund left in her honor. Her son, William C. Stroud, wanted to give his mother a lasting memorial that was more than stone; he wanted to provide a haven for elderly and handicapped individuals. The individuals staying at the home were considered guests and had their own private rooms with some sort of exposure to the outside. Visiting chaplains conducted services in the chapel located on the property. The Presbyterian Hospital managed the facility over the years and a registered nurse was on duty at all times.

(Photo from the Dorothy Reed Collection, courtesy Herb Fry)

▶ Around 1896, James Murphy, a day laborer from Ireland and his family, lived in Devon on Valley Forge Road in the home pictured. Before purchasing, the Murphy family rented the home for a number of years. According to area maps, the residence seems to have been in existence long before the Murphy occupancy. The present owners are the only residents outside the Murphy family to occupy the Devon home. The last Murphy to live in the home expressed to the present owners that the house was one of the first in Devon to have indoor plumbing installed.

S VALLEY FORGE RD

Wynburne Inn, Devon, Pa.

◀ The Wynburne Inn, near the Devon train station, was initially built for the Thorpes in 1887. The building was rented at one point to a Philadelphia woman who operated the place as a summer boarding home. Wynburne was located near the perimeter of Glassley Commons on the Old Lancaster Pike. The establishment was later named the Lincoln Inn and eventually, was destroyed by fire.

(Circa 1890s photo from the Dorothy Reed Collection, courtesy Herb Fry)

"Wynburne Inn" dining room.

Spiers Junior School

For Boys up to 16 years

A country school in the beautiful Main Line district of Philadelphia. Its purpose is sound training in habits of work for young boys. Its attractions of Equipment, Intimacy, Athletics, Scout Work, Gardening, Manual Training, Dramatics, Horseback Riding, etc., give fullest scope to all a true boy's tastes, and fulfill his parents' desires.

Full information on request. Visits are most welcome.

Mark H. C. Spiers
Headmaster
Box 256, Devon, Pa.

▲ The dining room at the Wynburne Inn.

◀ The Spier's Junior School was originally the Devon country home of the Clark Merchant Family in 1907.

▶ Established in 1942, the original Waterloo Gardens' greenhouse was situated on Lancaster Avenue in Devon. Over the years, the Devon location expanded its operation to Devon Boulevard and Berkley Road. Not seen since the resort era, Waterloo Gardens has brought back the liveliness to Devon Boulevard once again. The refreshing and uplifting feel of blooming flowers, garden activities, and holiday lights can only enlighten our imagination back to a time when the boulevard was Devon's main street for activity.

(Circa 1942 original greenhouse, courtesy Waterloo Gardens)

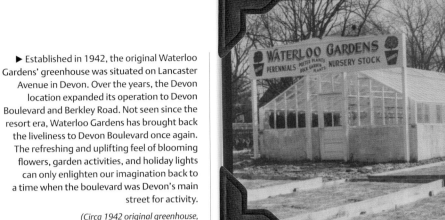

▲ ▶ The Pennsylvania Cattle Association held their annual cattle shows in Devon with entries from the across the country. 1912 marked the year for tuberculin testing of livestock, and many entries that year were banned from the Devon competition for not providing appropriate certificated documentation of disease-free stock. Then-President Howard Taft's White House cow Pauline, was barred from the show for lacking updated tuberculin certification, even though Taft was the honorary president of the Cattle Association. Local resident, William T. Hunter, was secretary for the Devon shows, and reported that $15,000 in prize money was awarded during the exhibition.

(Cattle Show advertisement courtesy Chester County Historical Society)

▶ William H. Wanamaker, Jr., of the department store family, played a part in organizing the fund that allowed proceeds from a scaled-down 1918 wartime show to be donated to the war's Emergency Aid Effort. Following the end of the war, the show continued its growth and popularity and selected the Bryn Mawr Hospital as the beneficiary for the donations.

(Circa 1916 photo courtesy Devon Horse Show and Country Fair, Inc.)

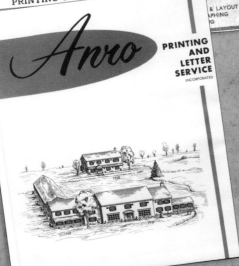

Announcing ... Our New Location

Frank J. Rossi, Builder

OFFICE SPACE AVAILABLE
(Anro Building)

AIR CONDITIONED SOUND CONDITIONED **AMPLE PARKING**

For the businessman who does not need a fulltime secretary - telephone answering and secretarial service is available.

Anro

Angelo & Rose Rossi

OFFSET PRIN
RAISED PRIN
ENGRAVING

PRINTING & LETTER SERVICE

& LAYOUT
RAPHING
G

Anro PRINTING AND LETTER SERVICE
INCORPORATED

▲ ◀ The site of the Campbell Greenhouses on Sugartown Road near Lancaster Avenue was cleared to make room for an apartment complex. Photo shows the bottom floors of the complex being built; smokestacks from the former greenhouses can be seen in the background.

A photo taken from Sugartown Road shows a rear view of the Main Line Drive-In movie screen. The drive-in's screen faced Lancaster Avenue and was demolished to make room for the Devon Square Shopping Center.

(Photos from the Dorothy Reed Collection, courtesy Herb Fry and Main Line Drive-In advertisement courtesy Suburban & Wayne Times)

◀ Devon residents, Angelo and Rose Rossi, started a home-based secretarial and duplicating service in the early 1950s. Their business, ANRO Incorporated, has grown into one of the largest printing and mailing companies in the Mid-Atlantic region.

The Philadelphia Inquirer

Published daily and Sunday. Entered as second class matter at the Postoffice in Philadelphia under Act of March 3, 1879

PHILADELPHIA, FRIDAY MORNING, APRIL 4, 1930 —— Copyright, 1930, by The Philadelphia Inquirer Co.

WEATHER—Fair

a b c d e

TWO CEN

GENERAL VIEW OF TRAGIC DEVON BLAST AND SOME REFUGEES

10 KILLED IN BLAS
AT DEVON PLAN
SCORES INJURE

Explosion in Fireworks Plant Spreads T in Three States; Factory and H Shattered, Seven Acres Blackene Flare-up; Windows Broken Ten Away; Four Seriously Hurt

Passengers on Train Nearby Cut Bruised; Bricks and Timber tered for Miles; Navy Depar and Marine Corps Aid Legion in Caring for Homeless

By JOHN M. McCULLOUGH

Seven blackened, pock-marked acres, where fires still smoulder beneath trees with gaunt and tered branches.

Ten blackened, hardly recognizable human b the comfortless and vague knowledge that someone blundered—and had taken the tragedy of his blunde eternity with him.

This is all that was known, and possibly all that is to know, about the series of terrific explosions yesterday blasted into minute, far-scattered atom eight frame and metal buildings comprising the pla the Pennsylvania Fireworks Display Company, Ind the outskirts of the village of Devon, between Old caster pike and Gulph road, sixteen miles from this

State police and highway patrolmen, township and county and State investigators sought vainly the day to search out some slightest clue which lead to the exact apportionment of the responsibilit the disaster which caused the death of ten pe critical injury to four others and more or less s injury to several score.

Their search led them to cots, where victims of the writhed in agony and w of death.

List of Dead and Wounded

JULY 1 SET TO FIX FINAL TUBE LEASE BY CITY WITH P. R. T.

Contract to Replace "Gentlemen's Agreement" on That Date

Power Taken From
by Council at Session After
Caucus

By HAROLD
Under the three
City Council yesterday
the uncertainties surrounding
Broad street subway o
year and a half by adopting a definite
programme. Its features

1. July 1, next, was fixed as the
final date for execution
enue-producing operating contract
with the Philadelphia
sit Company for
Grange street to
the present rent-fre
agreement."

2. An ordinance
gentlemen's agreement to the spr
below City Hall,
20, was amended so as to end it
July 1, and its provisions ratif
the Broad Street Subway Conference Board and autho
Mackey to negotiate a new lease
of the tube were

3. A committee
Councilman Charles
chairman of the
Committee; City Solicitor Augusta
Treak Ashton
Transit C. E. Myers was named to
deal with the P. R. T.
to the city of its share of the $2,-
000,000 income received by the
Broad street subway and pocketed
by the company since December
1928.

4. A resolution was adopted de-
claring the findings of the Broad
Street Subway Conference Board
could not be binding upon Council
and permitting the boar
its activities to the South Broad
street extension.

Agree in Caucus

The new Councilmanic programme
embodying these features was agreed
upon at a caucus held by the members
with Coleman J. Joyce, counsel for the
P. R. T.; City Solicitor Ashton and Director of Transit Myers in attendance.

► Firemen and fire trucks from Paoli, Berwyn, Wayne, Radnor, Bryn Mawr, and Ardmore immediately arrived at the scene. The area was blocked off and patrolled by state and township police with additional assistance from the cadets at the Valley Forge Military Academy. Cars traveling along Lancaster Pike were seized for public use to transport the seriously injured to Bryn Mawr Hospital. The response of the community to the needs of the victims was outstanding. Help arrived from a number of organizations and various sources. Physicians and nurses from Bryn Mawr Hospital arrived on the scene and set up a first aid station in one of the nearby damaged homes. Cots and blankets were made available by the Navy Department and Marine Corps in Philadelphia and transported to the area by a convoy of trucks.

(Photo courtesy The Historical Society of Pennsylvania)

RASKOB FACES QUIZ ON HIS $64,500 GIFT TO WET LOBBYISTS

Will Be Questioned by Senate Lobby Probers Today

Mitchell Opposes Jones Law
Modification in Letter to
House Judiciary Group

By GEORGE H. DIXON

Under the
this
the business of taking the census.
"Buy yourself under the coalpile,
false whiskers—the census-takers will
find you."

There just is no place where they
can't get at you
a submarine dodging swordfish and
with a huge sheet of paper and begin
asking you questions.

Even in jail, where ordinarily a man
is just a number and not an individual,
the gates and iron doors are not locked
against the enumerator. Witness the
procedure down in Moyamensing County Prison yesterday!

As the second day's activities in the

both afternoon and
evening sessions,
House, at Fourth and Arch streets.
She came to see—not to be seen. She
came to hear—not to be heard.

Hardly more than a score of persons in the city who saw the First
Lady of the Land recognized her

executive session today deferred decision on five measures placed before it
by the Wickersham Law Enforcement
Commission for tightening prohibition
enforcement and relieving court conges-

Continued on 17th Page, 2d Column

JURY FAILS TO AGREE
IN MAE WEST TRIAL

ton, executive director of the Philadelphia Business Progress Committee.
Fifty million dollars more plunged
into theatrical enterprises in this city
immediately, following the suggested
repeal of the Sunday blue laws were
the promise of the president of one
of the largest motion picture house
companies in the country.

pital and then discharged were:
Irvin Gill, of Green Tree, cuts
and bruises.
Joseph Walters, 125 Daly
street, Philadelphia; cuts.
Esther Borth, 4104 Spruce
street, Philadelphia; cuts.
Paul Manning, 1704 North Fif-
ty-second street, Philadelphia;
fractured rib.
Pellegrino di Massi, 726 Cath-

vania, New Jersey and Delaw
today; tomorrow, fair and w

Additional Weather Report on

MISSING PERSONS
MISSING since July, 1926, John Gil
64, and weight about 150 lbs.;
gray eyes. Anybody knowing
please notify Mrs. Mary C. Clements
mingo ave., Philadelphia.

LOST AND FOUND
LOST—Pocketbook, cont. salary
girl, on car No. 7 or 10th and Ch

WHERE MAIN FIREWORKS BUILDING WAS WIPED OUT BY BLASTS

FIREWORKS BLAST FELT LIKE QUAKE OVER WIDE AREA

Floors Tremble and Pictures, Dishes and Bric-a-brac Fall in Philadelphia Homes

WINDOWS RATTLE IN TRENTON AND BREAK IN GERMANTOWN

All the sensations of an earthquake were experienced in the Philadelphia area today.

The Devon fireworks plant blasts jarred the earth and buildings, and the population ran from homes and offices to see what was the matter. It was a half hour of intense excitement and suspense.

Effects of the terrific explosions were felt miles from the scene; in Trenton windows in the State House and other buildings rattled in the face of the blast.

City Hall and buildings in the centre of the city felt the shock plainly. Some persons said City Hall tower swayed slightly, and those in the Coroner's Court, directly beneath it, saw pictures wobble, and felt the floors shake.

"My glasses were shaken off my nose," said Louis Roth, clerk, describing the first two shocks and then the final explosion which sent him hurriedly to a telephone to learn what it was.

All parts of Philadelphia, especially the north and west portions, felt the blast. Germantown fairly heaved. "The Belgian blocks in the pavement just popped up and down," one woman there reported excitedly, "The children stood watching them for a

10 Ki In D

DEVON

▲ On Thursday, April 3, 1930, shortly after a 10 a.m. delivery of thirty kegs of black powder, The Pennsylvania Fireworks Display Company, Inc., exploded in a succession of three devastating blasts. The company was located on the north side of Old Lancaster Road in Devon, just north of the underpass where the road is crossed by the tracks. The blast was heard as far away as the State House in Trenton. Some southern New Jersey residents reported that they thought there had been an explosion at the DuPont plant located along the Delaware River.

The investigation into the cause of the explosion began immediately after the flames were extinguished. There were many expert opinions and theories, as well as countless conflicting statements, and rumors. The speculation was intense, possibly because this wasn't the only incident at the factory. According to a 1928 report of an earlier incident at the factory, an explosion caused a roof to blow off and fire at one of the buildings located on the property. There were no injuries, but the building was damaged beyond repair and was never rebuilt.

The jury for the case was unable to determine with certainty the cause of the explosion but concluded that the explosion, "probably was caused by the use of gas stoves for heating purposes in a building known as the workshop and the use of gas jets in the drying room." Adding, "the greatness of the explosions was caused by finished bombs and fireworks and the large quantity of black powder stored on the premises." The jury also recommended that "a stringent law be passed by the Commonwealth of Pennsylvania to cover the manufacture of fireworks, taking into consideration the location of plants and the quantity of raw and finished materials to be carried at one time, and that a plant of the kind be subjected to frequent and rigid inspection."

As reported in the Suburban and Wayne Times on August 29, 2002, "Tredyffrin Township buys 'fireworks tract' for $900,000." "The property, the site of a former fireworks manufacturer has remained vacant since a 1930 explosion …" "The township envisions a recreational facility with tot lots, benches, tennis and basketball courts, picnic and parking areas."

(Evening Bulletin courtesy Radnor Historical Society)

▼ Bits of red paper and other debris from the explosion were found as far away as Norristown. The concussion shattered windows in most buildings in Devon as well as in hundreds of homes from Wayne to Berwyn, and even some West Philadelphia buildings.

*(Photo courtesy
The Historical Society of Pennsylvania)*

The concussion shattered windows in most buildings in Devon as well as in hundreds of homes from Wayne to Berwyn, and even some West Philadelphia buildings.

▲ The Eagle Signal Tower, the control center for the interlocking switches on the Pennsylvania Railroad was in the line of destruction. The force from the blast knocked the signalman on duty from his chair, and overhead wires were strewn across the tracks. Flying glass from the train's windows injured many of the passengers waiting on board at the Devon train station. Pedestrians were knocked off their feet. Motorists on Lancaster Avenue were pushed off the road as if shoved by a sudden gust of wind.

(Photo courtesy The Historical Society of Pennsylvania)

◄ Many nearby homes were shaken to the point that the plaster came away from the walls exposing the lathe strips, and contents were tossed about as well as glass from shattered windows and broken china. Several homes and structures along Old Lancaster Road near the factory were either leveled or damaged beyond repair because the buildings were twisted and torn from their foundations.

(Photo courtesy The Historical Society of Pennsylvania)

◀ A view of houses along Old Lancaster Road in Devon near the former Devon Fireworks Factory. The home on the left was built around 1890 for William J. McCone, a carpenter from Ireland.

(Circa 1908 photo courtesy Stephen DiAddezio)

▲ The force of exploding fireworks and gunpowder left large holes, like shell craters, in the blackened earth. Some army veterans, who viewed the destruction site, compared what they observed to the "No-Man's Land" of World War I. All vegetation within the area of the blast was destroyed. Large trees were ripped apart with their branches shattered and torn off. Except for the office and one concrete foundation, there wasn't anything projecting more than two feet above the ground to indicate where buildings once stood.

*(Photo courtesy
The Historical Society of Pennsylvania)*

▶ Alexander Vardaro, shown sifting through debris, and his son Victor were owners of the company and escaped with minor injuries. Many employees were injured, but unfortunately, at least ten employees died in the devastating blast. Vardaro had been making fireworks in Devon for about twelve years starting in 1918 in the kitchen of workers' homes. The business then known as the Devon Fireworks Company experienced growth and expanded to include some additional small frame structures for factory production and storage on its seven acre site.

In 1930, the factory was renamed the Pennsylvania Fireworks Display Company, Inc.

*(Photo courtesy
The Historical Society of Pennsylvania)*

cenes of Disaster at Devon, Where Fireworks Blasts and Fire Wrought Havo

◄ A year before the explosion, the secretary of the nearby Neighborhood League sent a letter to the Bureau of Inspection of the Department of Labor in Harrisburg expressing concern over alleged employment of minors by the company and also communicated concerns regarding the numerous minor explosions. The secretary felt that there was a danger to both the children and the immediate area surrounding the factory. A reply from the Bureau of Inspection reported that inspections of the factory had shown that the proprietor of the plant was doing everything to comply with the law and that no evidence of violations of the law had been found.

The 1930-31 meeting minutes from the Radnor Fire Company reports that four of the explosion victims were under the legal working age for hazardous occupations.

(Public Ledger-Philadelphia courtesy Radnor Historical Society)

D'S-EYE VIEW OF STRICKEN AREA gives excellent idea of region which felt full force of explosion. Many injured were trapped in the houses

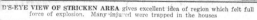

VALLEY FORGE CADETS rushed at double-quick to aid in work of rescue and foil vandals. Here they are lined up before splintered P. R. R. signal tower

INJURED VICTIM OF BLAST is loaded into one of man ambulances which helped carry the twoscore injured Bryn Mawr and Delaware County Hospitals

Y A SAMPLE OF DAMAGE wrought by fireworks blasts at Devon is contained in exterior view of building not far from razed factory, showing shattered windows emolished porch, and (below) interior view of same building, showing cracked walls

GROUP OF RESCUE WORKERS is shown here gathered near the shattered ruins of what was a comfortable small house before blasts in fire-

CAVED-IN ROOF was only part of damage suffered by this sturdy litt house under beating force of explosions which yesterday

1930 Devon Bocce Club

▲ In 1915, Italian immigrant workers settling in Devon founded the Italian Mutual Aid Society. The society, made up of mostly stonemasons, bricklayers, carpenters, electricians and landscapers, provided sick and death benefits to its members and their families. The club's benefits weren't always in a monetary form. Sometimes, just providing household support to families during a time of sickness or death, such as preparing meals or doing housework.

The society outgrew its original location, due to Devon's increase in population, and in 1930, the members pulled together and built another gathering place next door. That place was called the Devon Bocce Club where many played the popular Italian game. A banquet room was added in the 1940s for weddings, monthly homemade Italian dinners, and weekly dances.

The camaraderie of the two groups outweighed the cost of membership and in 1949 the two Italian organizations merged and the group was called the Italian Society and Bocce Club of Devon. Busy lives of the succeeding generations took its toll on the society. Even the swimming pool that was added in the 1960s couldn't attract the new family on the go of the 60s and beyond. Both buildings are no longer standing.

(Bocce Club and Lodge photos courtesy Herb Fry)

▼ Italian Mutual Aid Society Lodge, founded in 1915.

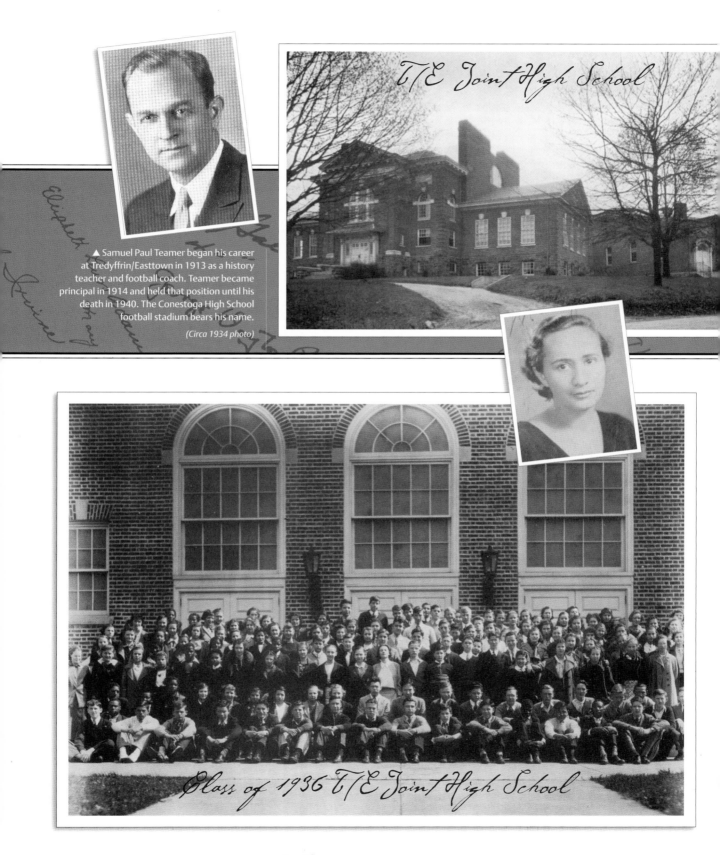

T/E Joint High School

▲ Samuel Paul Teamer began his career at Tredyffrin/Easttown in 1913 as a history teacher and football coach. Teamer became principal in 1914 and held that position until his death in 1940. The Conestoga High School football stadium bears his name.

(Circa 1934 photo)

Class of 1936 T/E Joint High School

Garnet and Gray

Fair T and E to thee our hearts ev-er turn-- where truth and ho-nor dwell and lights of know--ledge burn----Our Garnet and our Gray waves ev-er for thee-- where-er we go, we'll bear the own T and E--

1934 Football team

▶ The banquet for the 1952 T/E Joint High School football team.

1936 T/E Joint High School Band

HIGH SCHOOL

HIGH SCHOOL

Strawberry Kate

THE GARNET AND GRAY 1937

1937

HIGH SCHOOL

1936

The Devon Derby

Over 300 spectators attended the Devon Lawn Mower Derby on July 4, 1954, a first of this kind for suburban Philadelphia. Born from a friendly argument between two neighbors, the event was so successful that plans were made to hold future races at the Devon Horse Show grounds. Winners were awarded ribbons and cups, followed by a neighborhood picnic. The site of the race was on Steeplechase Road and Hunters Lane, and ironically, the Steeplechase road name reflects an event that was held on one of the early tracks designed for horseracing, which was at one time, located near the Devon Derby neighborhood.

(Photos courtesy Helen Sudhaus)

Henry Shute, day's winner, with cups.

The "Le Mans"

The

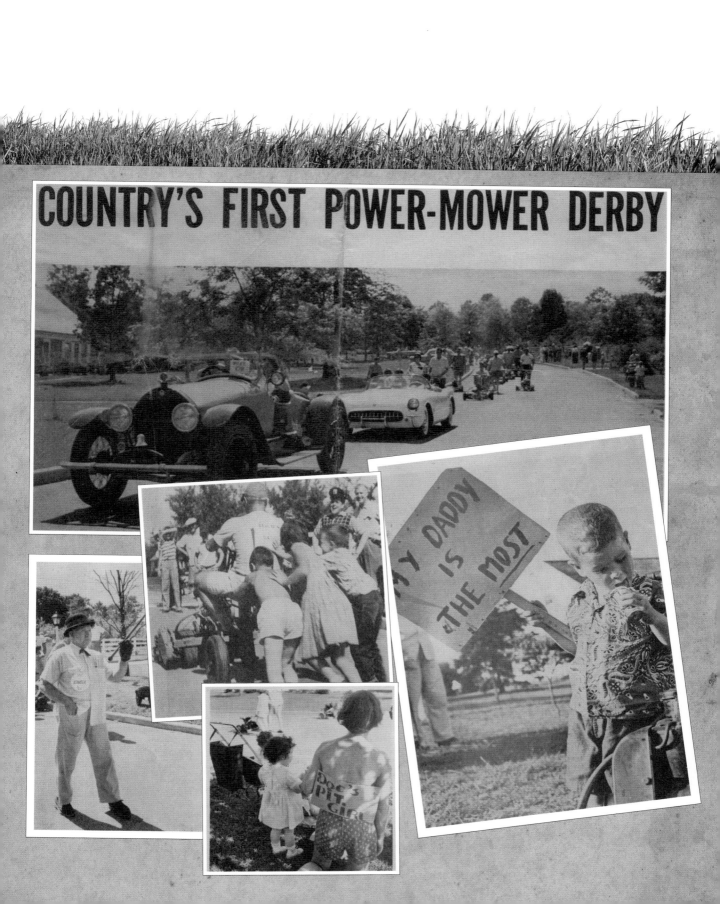

COUNTRY'S FIRST POWER-MOWER DERBY

IMAGES ALONG THE MAIN LINE

THE Main Line Airport hanger was located opposite the Penn State University entrance on Swedesford Road near Valley Stream Parkway in the Great Valley Corporate Center. Once situated within a farming community, the airport served the Main Line for more than 45 years. Charles Devaney became the first pilot to own and fly a plane in Chester County, and his family farm in the Great Valley provided a convenient location for him to take off and land. The farm was later sold to local inventor E. Burke Wilford, who converted the barn into a hangar. He painted PAOLI on the barn roof and laid out defined runways. In 1974, the Main Line Airport property was sold to Rouse and Associates, later known as Liberty Property Trust, to develop the Great Valley Corporate Center.

DATE 1936	AIRCRAFT FLOWN				TIME		ELAPSED FWD.		FROM
	License No.	MAKE	ENGINE	Class	TAKE-OFF	LANDING	HRS.	MIN.	
10/4	NC468V	Eaglet	Salmson	1				5	Paoli
10/11	NC468V	Eaglet	Salmson	1				15	Paoli
10/11	NC468V	Eaglet	Salmson	1			1	5	Paoli
10/13	NC468V	Eaglet	Salmson	1				5	Paoli
10/13	NC468V	Eaglet	Salmson	1				40	Paoli
10/15	NC468V	Eaglet	Salmson	1				20	Paoli
10/16	NC468V	Eaglet	Salmson	1				30	Paoli
10/20	NC468V	Eaglet	Salmson	1			1	2	Paoli
10/22	NC468V	Eaglet	Salmson	1				33	Paoli
						SOLO	4	5	Attested
Signature of Pilot	Samuel A. King, Jr.						Total Time Fw'd		

TO	No. Passengers	REMARKS
Local	SOLO	First solo flight.
Local	DUAL	Check flight.
Local	SOLO	Worked on landings.
Local	DUAL	Check flight.
Local	SOLO	Worked on landings
Local	SOLO	Worked on landings
Local	SOLO	Worked on approaches
Local	SOLO	Thirty minutes of cross country
Local	SOLO	Worked on landings

▲ *(Photo courtesy Stephen DiAddezio)*

Local pilots, Samuel King and Peter Cantrell, earned their pilot's license at the Main Line Airport. In the mid 1940s, both men attempted to establish a Malvern Airport nearby. Noise complaints from residents never allowed the airport to become fully operational.

(Samuel King's aeronautical treasures courtesy Mons King)

The airport transferred title of its operation over the years, and in 1936 E. Burke Wilford sold the property to aviation giant Curtis Wright Corp. of New York. Soon after, Charles Devaney came back to the airfield to form a partnership with close friend Nick Morris, a well-known flight instructor at the time, and established a business named Demorr Aeronautical Corp. Then, leasing the airfield, the new business had 89 acres of landing space and two training schools. In 1938, under President Franklin Roosevelt's civilian pilot training program, Demorr became home to a federally funded program that trained students between the ages of 18–27 to become pilots. Many students came from West Chester and Villanova Universities to obtain their licenses.

(Top and middle photos courtesy Stephen DiAddezio)

▼ The Main Line Airport was located opposite the Penn State entrance on Swedesford Road near Valley Stream Parkway.

▲ *(Photos courtesy Mons King)*

INSTRUCTION · CHARTER · SALES · SERVICE

DEMORR AERONAUTICAL CORPORATION

Owners and Operators

Main Line Airport, Paoli, Pa.

EASTERN DISTRIBUTOR FOR RYAN AIRPLANES

A Complete Instruction and Charter Service in Carefully
Maintained Modern Metal Airplanes

Plane Crash at Devon

On Wednesday afternoon, during the heavy rainfall, an Army training plane crashed near Waterloo and Exeter roads, Devon, on the estate of Percy Wilson and within 90 feet of his home,

May 26, 1943

The plane, which plummeted almost directly down between two clumps of trees shortly before 3 o'clock, buried its nose so deeply in the grassy plot that it required several hours for men from the airport and the State Motor Police barracks at Devon to bring out the flier's body.

▲ Charles "Pete" Conrad Jr., astronaut and commander of the Apollo 12 mission, had been known to cut grass on the runway at the Main Line Airport in exchange for flying lessons from Nick Morris. Conrad died in a motorcycle accident in California.

(Apollo 12 photo—Conrad pictured on the left courtesy Radnor Historical Society)

Devon Switching Station circa 1920

(Postcards and photos courtesy Stephen Diaddezio)

Trolleys and locomotives replaced the once popular mode of transportation, the Conestoga Wagon. The P&W Trolley Line that ended at Strafford has been transformed into a walking and bike trail.

PHILADELPHIA & WESTERN RAILWAY CO.

NORTHBOUND

Trains for
MAPLEWOOD ROAD
WEST WAYNE — SO. DEVON AVE.
SUGARTOWN ROAD
LANCASTER AVE. — STRAFFORD
Leave 69th STREET, PHILADELPHIA

WEEKDAYS		SATURDAYS		SUNDAYS	
A.M.	P.M.	A.M.	P.M.	A.M.	P.M.
5.12	2.53	5.12	3.13	5.35	4.15
5.42	3.13	5.42	3.33	6.18	4.33
6.03	3.33	6.03	3.53	6.45	4.53
6.26	3.53	6.26	4.13	7.15	5.13
6.48	4.13	6.48	4.33	7.45	5.33
7.04	4.34	7.04	4.53	8.15	5.53
†7.30	†4.53	†7.30	†5.13	8.45	6.13
†7.43	†5.13	†7.43	†5.25	9.15	6.33
7.55	†5.25	7.55	†5.37	9.45	6.53
8.13	†5.37	8.13	†5.55	10.13	7.13
8.33	†5.53	8.33	†6.13	10.33	7.33
8.53	†6.13	8.53	6.33	10.53	7.53
9.13	6.33	9.13	6.53	11.13	8.13
9.33	6.53	9.33	7.13	11.33	8.33
9.53	7.13	9.53	7.33	11.53	8.53
10.13	7.33	10.13	7.53		9.13
10.33	7.53	10.33	8.13	P.M.	9.35
10.53	8.13	10.53	8.33	12.13	9.53
11.13	8.33	11.13	8.53	12.33	10.13
11.33	8.53	11.33	9.15	12.53	10.33
11.53	9.10	11.53	9.35	1.13	10.53
	9.26		10.08	1.33	11.13
P.M.	9.55	P.M.	10.35	1.53	11.35
12.13	10.25	12.13	11.08	2.13	
12.33	10.55	12.33	11.35	2.33	A.M.
12.53	11.25	12.53		2.53	12.10
1.13	11.55	1.13	A.M.	3.13	1.00
1.33		1.33	12.08	3.33	
1.53	A.M.	1.53	12.55	3.53	
2.13	12.26	2.13	1.08		
2.33	1.05	2.33	2.02		
		2.53			
P.M.	A.M.	P.M.	A.M.	P.M.	A.M.

Express to [

† Express to Bryn Mawr then Local to Strafford.

The Sunday Schedule will be operated on Memorial Day, 4th of July, Labor Day, Thanksgiving, Christmas and New Year's.

— SUBJECT TO CHANGE WITHOUT NOTICE —

5/15/46   (over)

◀ A photo of the first trolley car on the Valley Forge line to reach Church and Main Streets in Phoenixville in 1915.

(Courtesy
The Historical Society of the Phoenixville Area)

In 1909, Thomas E. O'Connell, a promoter and builder of electric railways, began an effort that would provide a trolley line from Phoenixville to Valley Forge, and then through to Strafford, where it would connect to the P&W terminal, providing a direct link to the Main Line and Philadelphia.

O'Connell's effort was somewhat of a success, although it took a few years to solicit funds and additional support for his project. The trolley tracks' point of origin began in Phoenixville around 1912. A trolley amusement park called Valley Park opened about mid way between Phoenixville and Valley Forge along the new tracks. The laying of tracks continued to Valley Forge until a surprise glitch in O'Connell's perfect plan surfaced. Evidently, O'Connell, a talker in his own right, failed to verbally maneuver his way through the approval process with the Valley Forge Park Commission for granting a right-of-way for the construction of tracks through the park. The Phoenixville, Valley Forge & Strafford Electric Railway, for whatever reason, ended at Valley Park Road in Valley Forge.

(Certificates courtesy
The Historical Society of the Phoenixville Area)

◀ The remains of the Valley Park amusement and picnic park ticket booth.

(Photo courtesy
The Historical Society of the Phoenixville Area)

◀ Aerial photograph of Wayne in 1926.

(Courtesy Library Company of Philadelphia)

▼ Looking westbound on Lancaster Avenue in Wayne around 1890 and the same view in 2007.

(1890 photo courtesy Ernest C. Eadeh, Eadeh Enterprises)

GOOD HEALTH

IS THE MOST IMPORTANT THING FOR A LONG LIFE.

STOP AT

103 WEST LANCASTER AVE. WAYNE, PA.

AND EXAMINE THE BATTLE CREEK HEALTH BUILDER

NATHAN P. PECHIN

Electrical Contractor

▲ Circa 1928, Good Health advertisement.

(Courtesy The Lower Merion Historical Society)

▲ ▶ The Armitage School was a private school for girls in the early 1900s. The school was converted into apartment units.

(Postcard courtesy Margaret DePiano)

► The Wayne Opera House, Lyceum Hall, was built in 1871. Dramatic presentations, public lectures, and high school graduations were held there. A fire in 1914 destroyed the top floor.

(Circa 1880 and 1905 photos courtesy Radnor Historical Society)

▼ Circa 1928, Anthony Wayne Theatre advertisement.

(Courtesy The Lower Merion Historical Society.)

The Anthony Wayne Theatre

WAYNE

A Magnificent Palace of Amusement Destined to be a Source of Pride to the Main Line.

A Monument to the Loyalty and Good Will of a People and the Courage and Inspiration of its Founder—HARRY FRIED.

Circa 1950s aerial view of Devon-Strafford. Campbell's Greenhouses, well known for growing flowers, are pictured in the upper left corner.

(Aerial photo courtesy Lou DeStefano)

◄ Employed at the Campbell's Greenhouses in the early 1900s, award winner Joseph Isadore lived in the Devon-Strafford area. The greenhouses were known for prizewinning hydrangeas, poinsettias, and roses.

(Photo courtesy Melissa Purcell)

▶ The legacy of Miss Jeanne's Crossroads Tavern dates back to 1746 when it was a stage-coach stop and tavern for early travelers. Before acquiring the name Miss Jeanne's, the establishment was known as the New Centreville Hotel. Located off Route 202, at the Devon exit, the newly restyled old Miss Jeanne's continues its existence as a fashionable eatery.

(Photo courtesy Chester County Historical Society)

▲ Lou's Dairy Bar and Restaurant was the first establishment in the area to serve soft ice cream and pizza. Also originating at Lou's, the traveling lunch truck was a daily visitor at many local businesses. The popular eatery served the Main Line from 1951–1965.

(Circa 1957 photos courtesy Lou DeStefano)

▶ A 2007 view of the dairy bar's former location.

GALA OPENING
Saturday, April Fifteenth
Old Covered Wagon Inn
STRAFFORD, PA.

Platter Luncheons and Dinners

Sea Food a Specialty   Chicken and Waffles

Steak and Chop Dinners

All the Good Foods of the Season at Popular Prices

SPECIAL SUNDAY DINNER—75c, $1.00, $1.25

Ye Old Tappe Room has been arranged for the accommodation of our guests—Beer on draught, direct from wood—bottled Beer, Ale and Porter served with an inviting menu - - - -

ORCHESTRA AND DANCING
NO COVER CHARGE—MINIMUM AFTER 9.00 P. M. $1.00 PER PERSON

▲ The Old Covered Wagon Inn location as seen in 2007.

▲ ◄ For decades, the Old Covered Wagon Inn was a popular eatery and gathering spot along the Main Line. Transformed in appearance over its years of operation, the only original part of the structure was the center section (with chimney) that faced Lancaster Avenue. This section was once an outbuilding on a farm at the location. Records indicate that the original section of the inn was once used, not only for farming purposes, but also as a stagecoach stop and tavern on the then-named Lancaster Turnpike.

(Photo and advertisement courtesy Chester County Historical Society)

▼ Old Eagle School & Upper Gulph Road intersection in 1925.

(Photos courtesy Earnest C. Eadeh, Eadeh Enterprises)

Devon

◀ Aerial photograph of Devon in 1926.
(Courtesy Library Company of Philadelphia)

▼ Circa 1900 track side view of Devon train station.
(Courtesy Stephen DiAddezio)

Berwyn

▲ ▲ The Village of Berwyn circa 1910.
View looking towards Lancaster Avenue.

▲ Berwyn Post Office and bank circa 1920.
(Photo and postcard courtesy Stephen DiAddezio)

◀ Aerial photograph of Berwyn in 1926.
(Courtesy Library Company of Philadelphia)

Village of Berwyn, Pa.

BERWYN THEATRE, BERWYN, PA.

► In 1913, George Zimmerman, an auditor for the Pennsylvania Railroad, built the Berwyn Theatre on Cassatt Avenue. Zimmerman was related to Fred Zimmerman from the theatrical firm of Nixon & Zimmerman. The Berwyn Roller Rink occupied the building in 1955, and a farmers' market in 1978. In 1980, the old theatre was converted to an office building.

(Circa 1913 postcards of Berwyn Theatre and Cassatt Avenue courtesy Stephen DiAddezio)

CASSATT AVE, BERWYN, PA.

Berwyn Pharmacy, Berwyn, Pa.

▲ Dr. James and Mrs. Clara Aiken built the Aiken Drug Store in 1889. In 1910, Frank and Agnes Walker purchased the store and named it the Berwyn Pharmacy. Village children made memories of the Walker's soda fountain and ice cream parlor as they sat and enjoyed the treats on the five steps leading up to the drugstore door. The steps disappeared when the elevation of Lancaster Avenue was raised in the 1930s.

(Circa 1900 postcard courtesy Stephen DiAddezio)

◄ Built in the 1890s, "Langdale" was the home of Henry T. Coates in Berwyn. Coates was partner in the Philadelphia firm, Porter and Coates, publishers of children's books, and president of the first Devon Horse Show in 1896.

(Photo courtesy Library Company of Philadelphia)

► Isaac A. Cleaver started a mercantile business in an old store stand in Berwyn, which became too small for his growing business. In 1870, Cleaver built a new store on Lancaster Avenue across from Fritz's. Later, Cleaver's was destroiyed by fire by in 1890. Cleaver moved to a location across from the train station and called his new establishment, The Bee Hive Store.

(Circa 1890 photo courtesy Chester County Historical Society)

Fritz Lumber

▼ In 1863, Henry Fritz, a carpenter from Eagle (presently Devon-Strafford area) started the lumber and hardware business in Berwyn. During that same year, he married Mary Lobb. Fritz was killed in an accident at the Eagle station in 1870.

Preston Lobb, Mary's brother, operated the business until 1886 when Mary's oldest son William, was of age to take over the business.

(Fritz advertisement courtesy Lower Merion Hisotrical Society)

Bell Phone, Berwyn 8   Established 1886

WILLIAM H. FRITZ
BERWYN, PENNA.

COAL AND WOOD
GRAIN AND FEED
HAY AND STRAW
LUMBER AND BUILDING MATERIAL

Your Orders Will Have Prompt Attention
First-Class Goods at Market Prices.

SASH, DOORS and WOOD MOULDINGS

H. FRITZ,

Dealer in Lumber, Coal, Wood, Corn, Oats, Mill Feed, and Salt,
Calcined and Land Plaster, Cement, Terra Cotta Pipes, &c.
All kinds of LUMBER furnished at the shortest notice.

REESEVILLE,
Chester Co., Pa.

AMERICAN BRONZE CORPORATION

All Armed Forces trucks were equipped with an emergency repair kit produced by the foundry, which included replacement bronze bushings for parts of the truck that utilized them.

◄ In 1907, Jack Watson and Alfred Smith established the American Bronze Corporation. The foundry started out small, with two coke-fired furnaces and a small building in Berwyn. The business expanded, necessitating additional furnaces and space. "Non-Gran" was added to the foundry name early on as an attempt to reflect its finished product as being bearing bronze, which met government specifications for a non-granular quality bronze.

World War I brought more changes and an increase in production. All Armed Forces trucks were equipped with an emergency repair kit produced by the foundry, which included replacement bronze bushings for parts of the truck that utilized them. In addition to bronze products, automobile bearings were made at Berwyn, and around 1925, other metal types were introduced for production.

In 1927, unknown to most of us, the bearings used in Lindbergh's "Spirit of St. Louis" aircraft was produced at the Berwyn foundry for Wright Aeronautical Corporation of Paterson, New Jersey.

(Circa 1928 American Bronze advertisement and photos courtesy Stephen DiAddezio)

The Upper Bridge. Berwyn. Pa.

Wishing you many happy returns of the day your friend A

▲ Football players on Lancaster Avenue
at the lower bridge in Berwyn.
(Circa 1902 photo courtesy of Bill DeHaven)

▲▲ Circa 1900 postcard of the upper bridge
in Berwyn.
(Courtesy of Stephen DiAddezio)

BRYN MAWR 117

BRYN MAWR ICE

MANUFACTURING

AND

COLD STORAGE COMPANY

Lindsay Avenue and County Line Road

Bryn Mawr, Pa.

Mfg. Plants: Bryn Mawr, Wayne and

Berwyn, Pa.

— Capacity 120 Tons Per Day —

▶ Lancaster Avvenue and Midland Avenue
circa 1930s.

▲▲ Bryn Mawr Ice Co. in Berwyn.

(Courtesy Stephen DiAddezio)

On postcards (handwritten): *A view of North Berwyn from Berwyn Station P.R.R.*

Berwyn Station P.R.R.?

Berwyn Station P.R.R.

WM. H. DOYLE
NURSERYMAN AND CONTRACTOR
BERWYN, PENNA.

Roads built and repaired. Grading, Seeding, Tennis Courts, Swimming Pools and General Landscape work. Large trees furnished and transplanted without extravagance.

OVER FOURTY YEARS EXPERIENCE.

▲ *(All Berwyn train station postcards courtesy Stephen DiAddenzio)*

▶ The Springhouse Tavern was built in the early 1800s and was an ideal location for travelers of the old Lancaster Turnpike. The building was later used as a milk delivery depot and for manufacturing when the nearby Bronze factory expanded.

(Circa 1930s photo courtesy Chester County Historical Society)

128

▼ Early 1900s, view of Leopard Road at Lancaster Avenue, in Berwyn. Martin Potter built the stone home as pictured on Leopard Road.

(Photo courtesy Stephen DiAddezio)

▼ ▼ Lancaster Avenue looking west in the early 1900s.

(Photo courtesy Stephen DiAddezio)

Paoli

▲ ▲ A photograph of the Paoli Red Cross headquarters in 1918. According to records, the structure was once home to the old Jackson Tavern and Windmill House Tea Room. The Paoli branch of the Red Cross moved to Berwyn across from the firehouse on Bridge Avenue.

▲ In 1918, Camp Fuller, the United States Marine Corps training base was located on the west side of Cedar Hollow Road in Tredyffrin Township. In operation for only a few months, the camp provided shelter and training to a few hundred marines.

(Circa 1918 postcard and Camp Fuller photos courtesy Stephen DiAddezio)

◀ Aerial photograph of Paoli in 1926.

(Courtesy Paoli Library)

▲ *(Courtesy Suburban and Wayne Times, circa 1954)*

▲ ▶Circa 1900 view from Glenn Avenue
of the Daylesford train station.

(Courtesy Stephen DiAddezio)

▶Circa 1890s view of Valley Road
from the Paoli train station.

(Courtesy Stephen DiAddezio)

▼ Tredyffrin Country Club opened on June 1, 1918, with a limited membership of 200.

(Circa 1926 aerial photo courtesy The Library Company of Philadelphia)

STATEMENT

TREDYFFRIN COUNTRY CLUB
ROBERT T. BARNETT, Professional
PAOLI, PENNA. 3/26— 1925

Mr. Dr. Crane,

To Balance :	11/1 — 2 balls	1	50
Club Cleaning	" — 1 lesson 5 — 1 Sammy	3 6	— —
Club Repairs	18 — 2 balls	1	50
Golf Balls	13/21 — 2 "	1	50
Miscellaneous	" — 1 Lesson	2	—
	13/22 — 1 new shaft	2	50
	Course of Lessons	25	—
	" " " (Mrs. Crane)	5	—
	1 Driver	7	—
	1 Brassie	7	—
	1 spoon	7	—
	1 mashie	6	—
	1 doz. repaints	4	—
	#	79	00

Make all checks payable to Robert T. Barnett

Tredyffrin Country Club

Limestone quarries were Howellville's most profitiable resource, dating back to the late 1700s and up through the 1900s. In 1934, Frances H. Ligget, a local historian, organized a cleanup effort with the support of the Valley Forge branch of the Farm and Garden Association for the village of Howellville. The depressed era took a toll on the village and its citizens. Warner Company of Cedar Hollow supplied whitewash, and trucks from the quarry hauled away loads of debris. Cannon balls from the Revolutionary days were found under layers of trash.

The communities in the area came together during a depressed time to assist in the cleanup effort that afforded the residents of Howellville to regain their pride in refreshed surroundings.

(Circa 1934, photos courtesy the Paoli Library, Frances Ligget Collection)

▶ The Trenton cut-off railroad tunnel in 1934.

(Photo courtesy the Paoli Library, Frances Ligget Collection)

...communities in the area came together during a depressed time to assist in the cleanup effort that afforded the residents of Howellville to regain their pride in refreshed surroundings.

▲ ◀ A view of the intersection at Howellville and Swedesford Roads in 1934.

(Photos courtesy the Paoli Library, Frances Ligget Collection)

▲ A view of the intersection of Howellville and Swedesford Roads in 2007. The community closed its quarries years ago, but the area continues to thrive with large business and residential complexes encircling their once tiny village of Howellville.

THE ENGLISH CONNECTION

ÐEVON, in Pennsylvania, was named after England's resort town, according to records. However, there may be more of a connection other than the resort one. The American merchants, Coffin and Altemus, had acquired not only a taste for the architectural style and grandeur of buildings in England, but also had inherited the popular European entrepreneurial trend of purchasing and developing land which was occurring at that time.

▶ **Compare The Two**
England's Peek House holds a striking resemblance to the former Devon Inn by its size and roofline architectural characteristics of dormer window gables and multiple chimneys.

In 1868, Englishman Sir Henry Peek, a wealthy tea and grocery merchant and Member of Parliament for Wimbledon, purchased Rousdon, a working estate parish (village) in Devon, England. Around 1878, he built a mansion on the property that seems to have a striking resemblance to the old Devon Inn.

The size and character of the English estate was befitting those who enjoyed luxury and financial wealth on a grand scale. Complete with an observation tower that once served as Sir Henry's Justice Room, the estate's mansion had plenty of room for servants, bedrooms for family and guests, a long main hall that doubled as a bowling alley, a porte-cochère for protection from the elements, and outbuildings that consisted of a church, school, store, dairy, museum and stable. At one time the mansion and outbuildings could accommodate up to 600 village people.

continued

Apparently, when Sir Henry purchased the village, his acquisition included the leadership and growing opportunities that followed. The estate later transitioned into a school called All Hallows School and eventually became known as the Peek House, a renowned country estate and resort located in a park-like setting in Rousdon, between the East Devon and West Dorset borders in Devon, England.

Resembling America's former Devon Inn, not only in style and luxury, the Peek House seems to hold a very similar past of occupants and communal interests. Sir Henry, a wealthy merchant, purchased the English village and built a mansion that not only served as a home for his family, but also as the central location for business activities of his village. Since it wasn't customary to purchase a town in America, Devon's developers, Coffin and Altemus, who were also wealthy merchants, first acquired the land, then established the town around their newly-built inn. The inn not only provided a service to accommodate wealthy guests, but also served as the town center for their growing community. Following the resort era and a series of transactions, the inn transformed into various private schools.

▲ Devon Inn

The trend of purchasing and developing land wasn't new to the Coffin family. The Coffin ancestry places the family lineage in Massachusetts, back to the mid-1600s when Tristram and Peter Coffin, were included as original purchasers of the Massachusetts island of Nantucket in 1659. Tristram Coffin, then-considered to be the island's patriarch, wanted his acquisition to be a place where his family, which grew extensively, could live around him while the island was developed as a seaport. Peter Coffin was known at that time to be an individual of great financial wealth. Genealogy records of the Coffin (Coffyn) surname reflect an ancestral connection to Devon England as descendants of Christopher Peake. ◄

(Peek House photo/s courtesy Warwick Bergin, Peek House, Devon England)

SOURCES

- American Premier Underwriters, Inc.: photograph
- Ancestry.com; Rootsweb.com; other genealogy websites
- Chester County Archives, West Chester, PA: deeds & maps research
- Chester County Days; Village of Berwyn, PA, Barbara Fry
- Chester County Historical Society, West Chester, PA: photographs; newspaper clipping files; research
- Conversations with Conrad Wilson & Bebe Pancoast regarding Cockleburr Cabin
- Devon Horse Show & Country Fair, Inc.: photographs; images; research
- Dorothy Reed Photograph Collection
- Easttown, Old in History Young in Spirit (1704-2004) by C. Herbert Fry
- Easttown Township & Hilltop House, Devon, PA: research; images & photographs
- Franklin Maps, King of Prussia, PA
- The Historical Society of Devon, England: research
- The Historical Society of Pennsylvania, Philadelphia, PA: photographs; research
- The Historical Society of the Phoenixville Area, PA: photographs; research
- The History of Nantucket by Alexander Starbuck, 1924
- Library Company of Philadelphia, PA: photographs; research
- The Lower Merion Historical Society, Bala Cynwyd, PA: advertisement booklet & research
- National Register of Historic Places: Waterloo Mills Historic District; Wetherby-Hampton-Snyder-Atlee-Wilson Log Cabin (Cockleburr); Old Eagle School
- Paoli Library, PA: Reminiscences, Great Valley Days by Frances H. Ligget; photographs & research
- Peek House & Resort, Devon, England: photographs
- The Radnor Historical Society, Wayne, PA: Bulletin, Vol. VII #5 & other bulletins; research; photographs; Main Line Life article (Pete Conrad, Jr. & Main Line Airport)
- Suburban & Wayne Times: research; images
- Tredyffrin/Easttown History Club Quarterly documents:
  - Anne H. Cook, Furness Barns in Tredyffrin, Vol. XXII #4
  - Anne H. Cook, Reports on Chesterbrook Farm; West Chester Daily News, Vol. XXIII #I

- Robert M. Goshorn, Where Champions Meet, Devon Horse Show & Country Fair, Vol. XXXII #3
- Ruth D. L. Mansley, The Paoli Branch of the American Red Cross, Vol. V #1
- Sara Nuzum, Isaac Cleaver & Bee Hive Store, Vol. XIII #3
- The Sign of the Fox, Vol. I #4
- Samuel Paul Teamer Vol. III #4
- William Tubbs, Cathcart Home, Vol. X #3

- West Country Studies Library, Devon, England: research
- Additional Photo/Image Credits:
  - John H. Ansley Postcard (Devon Manor) pg. 42
  - Vincent Benedict, Devon streetscape sketches on pgs. 80,81
  - Chester County Historical Society, pg. 127 (top & bottom photo)
  - Devon Horse Show & Country Fair, pgs. 28, 29, 30, 31
  - Ray Harshbarger, pg. 74 (American Indian Historian)
  - Lower Merion Historical Society (Wm. H. Doyle advertisement) pg. 128
  - Mons King, pg. 104 (lower right plane photo) pg. 105 (lower left plane photo)
  - Suburban & Wayne Times (plane crash article) pg. 105 (Devon Hobby Shop pg. 142)
  - Union Pacific League, pg. 66 (Historians)
  - Valley Forge (excerpt from brochure) pg. 76

◀ A 1930 view of the pool that William T. Hunter built on his property for the children of Devon.

(Photo courtesy ANRO Inc.)

▼ Circa 1890s view of Warren Avenue in Berwyn.

(Photo courtesy Stephen DiAddezio)